JUSTICE?
Stories of Famous Modern Trials

JUSTICE?

STORIES OF
FAMOUS MODERN TRIALS
LEONARD GRIBBLE

RAVEN BOOKS
ABELARD-SCHUMAN
NEW YORK • LONDON • TORONTO

Library of Congress Catalog Card Number: 72-157986
ISBN 0 200 71838 x
Published by arrangement with Arthur Barker Ltd., London

LONDON	NEW YORK	TORONTO
Abelard-Schuman	Abelard-Schuman	Abelard-Schuman
Limited	Limited	Canada Limited
8 King St. WC2	257 Park Ave. So.	228 Yorkland Blvd.

An Intext Publisher

Printed in the United States of America

TO ALL WHO ROUNDLY CONDEMN INJUSTICE
AND BITTERLY DECRY LACK OF JUSTICE

CONTENTS

AUTHOR'S PREFACE

The twelve trials that provide the subjects for the present volume cover the years from just before the twentieth century until the close of its seventh decade.

All, in their different categories and dramatic impacts, made legal and courtroom history and not a few served to shock and even educate public opinion, which is often salutary and timely, a development to be applauded so long as justice is served.

Of course miscarriages of justice occur, but it is in those courts where they occur that the error, in retrospect, can be seen for what it is. Further, it is often in the power of the judges themselves to ensure that the wrong is righted.

This is not the least reason why stories of famous trials hold an intense interest for the inquiring mind. The human dramas enacted in a courtroom can always be viewed with personal interest, for it takes little imagination to picture one's own involvement in like circumstances. It is this innate personal appeal that gives to courtroom dramas both the pathos that stirs one's sympathy and the sense of outrage that frequently demands condemnation. Yet both sentiments are aroused merely by the presentation of facts by specialists in advocacy.

The reader of such courtroom dramas is always free to step into the role of a secret juryman and to take part, as it were, while remaining in the wings of a trial that often moves to its climax with the calculated overtones of suspense and conflict usually to be found in a carefully plotted stage drama.

To avoid creating a false sense of continuous courtroom atmosphere and sameness in presentation, the chapters have been designed as stories centred on the events that gave rise to the trials. In this way it is hoped that the reader will not only share in the courtroom drama itself, but find additional interest in the lives and emotions of people who either created the circumstances that finally overwhelmed them, or were caught up in the coils of mystery and tragedy just as any reader might be.

In such conflicts involving conscience and moral values, as well as the results of violence and villainy, the sheep are often fortunately discernible from the social goats. But it is never wise to forget the existence of the occasional black sheep.

When discovered and recognized for what he is, he can usually provide a stimulated excitement by his very unique quality, which is what often makes some spectacular villain not only formidable but superficially attractive. Among the sheep and goats appearing in the following pages some of the former are of noticeably varying shades of fleece, including deepest black. It remains for the reader to find them and recognize them.

JUSTICE?
Stories of Famous Modern Trials

THE RIDDLE OF THE BORDEREAU

October 15, 1894, was a crisp autumn day in Paris. In the Avenue du Trocadéro, on the right bank of the Seine and not far from where Monsieur Eiffel's great tower had stood for five years on the opposite bank, a neatly dressed man left his home and began walking smartly down the street in the direction of the Rue Saint-Dominique. He was dressed in well-cut everyday clothes, not in uniform, and the only clue to his being an officer in the French Army was his military carriage and the brisk pace at which he moved. In the Rue Saint-Dominique was the building that housed the French Ministry of War. The man stepping along in the autumn sunshine was due there to attend what was politely termed a general inspection. Which meant that he was on the carpet and required to account for his past behavior.

Although when in uniform he wore the insignia of a captain of the General Staff, his official appointment had been qualified as that of a *stagiaire*. This meant that he was actually serving a period on probation. He had been appointed to the post on January 1 of the previous year, and had conducted himself in exemplary fashion. But now he was under a cloud. He was a man with enemies although he had not gone out of his way to be offensive to anyone.

His name was Alfred Dreyfus. He had been born in Alsace, in the town of Mulhouse, and had only a few days before celebrated his thirty-fifth birthday.

One detail segregated Captain Dreyfus from most of his

13

brother officers. He was a Jew. This difference in religious background was to a very considerable extent responsible for his taking that walk to attend the general inspection dressed in the clothes of a civilian. Quite a few officers on the French General Staff at that time were anti-Semitic. They distrusted Jews as being too international-minded, and for that reason considered their patriotism might well be less than sufficient for a Frenchman devoted to his country.

Dreyfus understood the disadvantage his Jewish faith afforded him in his chosen career, but he was a man with an uncomplicated mind who knew how he wished to spend his life. As an artillery officer, before being promoted to a Staff post, he had been happy and contented to await promotion when it came.

Her certainly had no wish to enter the offices of his family's large textile mills, which at that time were very prosperous. His family was one of considerable substance. It was also very respected in Mulhouse.

But Mulhouse was a great distance away that October day when Alfred Dreyfus's life was to change abruptly.

On the walk to the Ministry of War the captain who had been ordered to appear at the "general inspection" in civilian clothes had plenty of time to review what had been his life up to that October morning. In 1889 he had married. His wife had been Lucie Hadamard. She had presented him with two children, a boy Pierre and a girl Jeanne. As a captain in the Fourteenth Regiment of Artillery the children's father had lived quietly but without having to rely on his army pay, for he received a handsome income from the Mulhouse mills.

When he had appeared before General Bonnefort, head of the selection committee, for entrance to the École Supérieure de Guerre, as the French Staff College was known, Dreyfus had been well aware of the General's anti-Semitic feelings. His comments had been sharp, and when the applicant left the interview he was in no doubt that General Bonnefort's report on him would not be faborable.

It wasn't.

On the list of applications in the General's possession when Dreyfus confronted the selection committee, his name was in third place. Shortly after the interview it was placed ninth.

However, fortunately for the applicant other members of the selection committee had entertained higher opinions about his capabilities as an officer and his qualities for an appointment to the General Staff. So he had been received as a probationary Staff officer with the disapproval of General Bonnefort.

What the officer in civilian dress did not know as he made his way to keep his appointment was that three months before, in the summer of that year of 1894, an apparently anonymous letter had been addressed to the German military attaché in Paris, Colonel von Schwartzkoppen. Max von Schwartzkoppen was a popular figure in the French capital and made friends easily. When that anonymous letter disappeared from his office in the German Embassy and arrived mysteriously in the possession of a French major of what was called the Statistical Section of the Ministry of War, a scandal was about to break.

The French major, whose name was Herbert Joseph Henry, was a veteran risen from the ranks who had seen action in Africa with one of the colonial regiments of Zouaves. Although he had not passed through the Staff College, he had been given a post in the Deuxième Bureau because General de Boisdeffre, Chief of the General Staff, thought highly of him as an Intelligence officer. The letter that came so mysteriously into Henry's hands was written in French on very thin paper that rustled as one held it. It had no date and was not signed.

Its contents ran:

Although I have not heard whether you wish to see me I am sending you, sir, some interesting information:

(1) A description of the hydraulic brake of the 120 and how it is operated.

(2) A note on the covering troops. (The new plan contains some changes.)

(3) A note on alterations in artillery formations.

(4) A note relative to Madagascar.

(5) The proposed manual for field artillery (March 14, 1894).

It has been very difficult to procure the last-named document and I can keep it for only a few days. The Minister has sent a number to the corps, for which they are responsible. Every officer who has one must return it when the manoeuvres end. So if you will take what you find useful and have the original ready for me, I will collect it. Unless you prefer that I should copy it *in extenso* and send the copy to you.

I am now leaving to attend the manoeuvres.

This letter, obviously the work of a spy in the pay of the Germans and a traitor to France if it was genuine, seemed to be equally obviously the work of an artillery officer. The reference to the 120 mm howitzer in such a familiar way pointed to as much. So did the information about the artillery manual.

How this letter, which became famous by its French description of *bordereau,* or schedule, ever came into Henry's hands is still largely a mystery. The *bordereau* was understood by a good many high-ranking French officers to have been found ripped into quarters lying in Max von Schwartzkoppen's wastepaper basket. The person who found it was a Madame Bastian, employed as a cleaning woman in the German Embassy, who was said to have been employed by Major Henry. Henry put the torn letter together, pasted the quarters to another sheet of paper, and showed the result to his superiors.

It confirmed the worst suspicions of certain officers on the French General Staff, who had complained that for some time secret military information had found its way into the hands of both the Germans and the Italians. The persons believed to be responsible for employing a traitor were Colonel Max von Schwartzkoppen and the Italian Military Attaché, Colonel Panizzardi, both of whom were known to be able and very keen officers.

For some time Major Henry of the Deuxième Bureau's Statistical Section, which devoted its time to what would be called today counterespionage, had been trying to learn who on the French Staff was the mysterious contact with the German and Italian Embassies. Two civilians used to gather discarded scraps of paper were a man named Brucker and the woman Bastian.

Later Dreyfus, the man whose career was to be wrecked by the notorious *bordereau,* was to give a very different version of how the letter came to be passed on to the General Staff. According to Dreyfus, Madame Bastian did not find the torn pieces. She knew nothing about the letter. On the other hand, Brucker had become friendly with the concierge at the German Embassy. He had induced the concierge to let him into Max von Schwartzkoppen's office, where he had gone through a secret file and extracted the letter.

Brucker took the letter to Henry, who, Dreyfus later claimed, recognized the handwriting. It was the writing of a Major Marie Charles Ferdinand Walsin-Esterhazy, a friend of Henry's who was at the time serving with a French infantry regiment. Acting on impulse to protect his friend, Henry tore up the traitorous *bordereau*, but before it could be completely destroyed was stopped by Brucker.

"If you don't report this letter, Major Henry," said the alarmed agent of the Deuxième Bureau, "I will."

So the four pieces were pasted together and taken to Colonel Sandherr, the Bureau's chief, who promptly commended Henry for recovering the letter. The pasted-up letter was photographed and the copies were shown in confidence to high-ranking officers and officials of the War Ministry. They were asked if they recognized the handwriting. None did.

A colonel on the General Staff insisted that the letter had been written by both an artillery officer and one of the probationers. On the official list at that time only one name belonged to an artillery officer who was a probationer.

Captain Alfred Dreyfus.

The name of the colonel who made this discovery was d'Aboville. He was known to be vociferously anti-Semitic. When he mentioned the result of his checking to his chief, Colonel Fabre, head of the Army bureau responsible for transport and communications, word was sent to General Mercier, the Minister for War. The Minister was also informed that the handwriting on the *bordereau* resembled that of Captain Dreyfus.

Auguste Mercier was a worried man when this scandal was dropped into his lap. He was a politician with reason to fear the opposition of his day. He had Monsieur Gobert, a handwriting expert employed by the Banque de France, compare a sample of Dreyfus's writing with the *bordereau*. The bank expert's opinion didn't help the harassed Minister.

"There is a superficial similarity," he declared, "but in my opinion they are not the work of the same hand."

General Mercier then called on the services of the famous

Alphonse Bertillon, whose anthropometrical system of criminal identification made him pre-eminent in his own field in France. Bertillon, however, was not an expert in handwriting techniques and graphology, and he assumed that what was required of him was not an independent opinion, but confirmation of one already formed. So he obliged, as did a number of other alleged experts.

So far as Dreyfus was concerned the die was cast.

He was summoned to the "general inspection" on October 15, and arrived in due course to find himself confronting Major Mercier du Paty de Clam, of the bureau responsible for military operations and training, Police Commissaire Cochefort and his secretary, and Monsieur Gribelin, the War Ministry's archivist. What happened then was a piece of play-acting.

The major had a large bandage round his right thumb, which was not hurt. He asked Dreyfus to take down a letter at his dictation, and while the artillery captain was still writing the major broke off his dictation to declare, "Captain Dreyfus, I arrest you in the name of the law. You are accused of high treason."

It was pompous and comical. It was also exceedingly tragic, for as Dreyfus jumped to his feet protesting, he was seized and his pockets emptied. Then, assured that the man under arrest was not armed, the major questioned him closely for two hours, and throughout that time kept urging Dreyfus to confess his guilt, something the indignant captain refused to do, for he stoutly maintained his innocence and denied all knowledge of the *bordereau*.

A way out of a growing dilemma was suggested when Dreyfus was shown a loaded revolver.

"If you wish to use it, you will be left alone," he was told.

"I have no reason for using it on myself," retorted the angry and dismayed captain.

"Then I cannot help you," said the major, who had bungled his task of getting either a confession or a corpse which would have been even more acceptable.

Dreyfus was taken to the Cherche-Midi military prison and lodged in a cell well away from other prisoners. Kept in solitary confinement for three days, refused the opportunity of writing to his wife or his friends on the express orders of the Minister, he was nearly driven out of his mind. Only the consideration shown him by the prison governor, Major Ferdinand Forzinetti, who could not believe in Dreyfus's guilt, helped to sustain him.

Major Paty de Clam used those three days to search the Dreyfus home and to terrify Madame Dreyfus. Although unsuccessful in the first, the major was certainly successful in the second. But reducing a scared woman to tears was not enough. The major went to the prison and demanded that the governor supply him with some bright lamps with which he could "unhinge" the prisoner. The governor refused to help him, and several prison visits by the major, during which the prisoner was harassed and urged to provide a confession, resulted in no easy way out for those responsible for Captain Dreyfus's arrest.

Ten days after the major's request for bright lamps had been refused, a letter appeared in *Libre Parole* of October 28. It said that Captain Alfred Dreyfus had been arrested on a charge of espionage, and the informed writer stated: "The story is that he is travelling, but that is a lie told because they want to hush up the affair. All Israel is stirring."

The writer of the letter gave his name simply as Henry.

The next day the Paris press reported that an important arrest on a charge of espionage had been made. What became known as the Dreyfus Affair was suddenly no longer a secret. To satisfy critics of the way the arrest had been handled, a court-martial was arranged.

It opened on December 19. The well-known French advocate, Maître Charles Demange, had been asked by the prisoner's brother Mathieu to undertake the defense of a prisoner who had been refused permission to write to his wife for seven weeks and was still forbidden to see his family.

Unknown to Demange or the prisoner, General Mercier had placed before the members of the court-martial a number of documents hat had no bearing on the case but which were damaging to the prisoner. One of them was an item of correspondence between Max von Schwartzkoppen and Colonel Panizzardi referring to maps of Nice sold them by "that rogue D——." It was not hard to supply the rest of the missing name beginning with D, in the circumstances, though appearances lied. The name was Dubois, not Dreyfus. Some of the papers which influenced the court were later burned on the orders of General Mercier. Meantime, however, they had done what was expected of them.

On December 22 Dreyfus was found guilty by the court-martial. The sentence was severe. The artillery officer was to be cashiered, then to be imprisoned for the remainder of his life.

The real persecution of Alfred Dreyfus was about to begin.

Christmas passed and on January 5, 1895, a large crowd collected outside the École Militaire, where an escort comprising an officer and four soldiers led Dreyfus into the center of the large courtyard. An order rang out, boots stamped on the cobblestones, and then the sentence was read aloud.

Dreyfus found his voice and shouted.

"Soldiers," he cried, "an innocent man is being degraded."

An officer approached him and tore from his uniform his badges of rank, buttons, and ornamental stripes, all of which had been loosened in readiness. They were flung on the ground. The prisoner's sword was broken in two across the officer's knee.

"I am innocent!" shouted Dreyfus.

Another command rang out, and he was forced to march in his tatters around the large square while the crowd howled abuse at the man they believed to be a traitor in the pay of France's potential enemies. Then Dreyfus was handcuffed and put into a prison vehicle to be taken away and photographed as a felon and given a number in place of a name.

He was allowed two visits a week from his wife, but these did not continue for long, for on January 17, in the middle of the night, he was removed from Paris. He was taken to a ship that carried him across the Atlantic to the French penal settlement of Devil's Island. After a false report reached Paris that he had attempted to escape, he was ordered to be placed in irons each night. This harsh treatment continued for thirty-four nights before the order was cancelled. But no matter how harsh the treatment, his spirit could not be broken. He maintained his innocence and forced himself to be patient, knowing that back in France his brother and friends would be working on his behalf.

It was Colonel Picquart, a member of the court-martial, who came by the first clue that was to establish that an innocent man had been found guilty. Madame Bastian had continued filching scraps of paper from Max von Schwartzkoppen's wastebasket, and among some she recovered in March 1896 were the torn-up pieces of an express letter known as a *petit bleu*. The writer had apparently had second thoughts about sending it. When the pieces were put before Colonel Picquart he saw that they comprised a letter written to Major Esterhazy at an address in the Rue de la Bienfaisance. The writer had penned:

> I am awaiting a fuller explanation than you gave me the other day. I beg you to give it me in writing so that I can decide whether to continue my association with House of R.

There was no signature save a single initial C, which was known to be used by the German Military Attaché. Colonel Picquart, a man who had not personally been convinced about the guilt of the branded traitor on Devil's Island, had inquiries made about Esterhazy and learned that he was a husband who had squandered his wife's fortune, a compulsive gambler, and a man in debt to moneylenders. About the time he learned the facts about Esterhazy, he also heard from another source that the German General Staff had been astonished at the court-martial of Dreyfus, for they had never heard of him. A Staff officer in Berlin had admitted that Colonel von Schwartzkoppen was paying money to a French officer, but his name was certainly not Dreyfus. It was enough, Colonel Picquart decided, for him to make further cautious inquiries about Dreyfus. He came to the conclusion that the prisoner on Devil's Island had been unjustly convicted.

He approached General de Boisdeffre with all the documents he had compiled, including the notorious *bordereau* and the *petit bleu*. The Chief of the General Staff sniffed the odor of a fresh scandal and turned Picquart over to his deputy, General Gonse, who at once demanded that nothing should be done to link Esterhazy with Dreyfus.

The colonel pointed out coldly that the honor of the French Army was involved and reminded Gonse that Mathieu Dreyfus and others were working relentlessly to try to establish the prisoner's innocence.

All Gonse said was, "We can't reopen the Dreyfus case."

To make sure that Picquart was no longer available to become a probing nuisance, he was dispatched to Tunisia. Before he left France there was another development. Picquart had told a lawyer friend named Leblois of his belief in Dreyfus's innocence and why, and Leblois took up the matter with some members of the Senate.

By now the newly promoted Colonel Henry had produced a fresh letter, this time from Colonel Panizzardi, which seemed to confirm Dreyfus's guilt. But this letter was proved to be a crude forgery. So it was clear that interests were at work to keep Dreyfus in his convict's cell thousands of miles from France. But the whole business of intrigue and double-dealing came into the open when Mathieu Dreyfus published a letter to the Minister in which he accused Esterhazy of being a spy and the writer of the *bordereau*.

By this time all France was in an uproar about the case.

Esterhazy was court-martialled in January 1898, but the vital evidence of Colonel Picquart was not made public and Esterhazy was acquitted.

It looked as if the whole case had gone back where it started, but two days after acquittal the brilliant writer Émile Zola published in the newspaper *L'Aurore* his famous letter addressed to the French President and headed *J'Accuse*. In it he accused the members of the court-martial of December 1894 with breaking the law by obtaining a verdict on secret evidence while concealing evidence that should have been made public.

This letter produced a violent reaction. Both Zola and the publisher of *L'Aurore*, Monsieur Perreux, were accused of defaming the members of the court-martial, whom Zola had named, including four Generals, Billot, Mercier, de Boisdeffre, and de Pellieux. Colonel Paty de Clam, as he now was, also came in for dishonorable mention. Zola and his publisher had to stand trial. The ordeal lasted from February 7 until the 23rd. It was stormy as only a notable French trial can be. Such advocates as Georges Clemenceau and Labori kept the legal pot boiling, but at the close the jury took only thirty-five minutes to bring in a majority verdict of guilty. When applause broke out in the public galleries, Zola rose and pointed to them.

"They are cannibals!" he shouted.

He was sentenced to a year in jail and a fine of three thousand francs. His publisher was also sent to prison for four months and fined the same amount.

Zola had lost a case, but not a cause. For during the lengthy trial the story of Alfred Dreyfus had been pared to the bone. The truth was no longer clothed in false accusations. The first result of this airing of the truth was obtained when Zola's case was heard by the Appeal Court, which quashed the verdict of the court that had found him guilty. However, when a second trial was ordered, Zola's friends told him to get out of the country until the Dreyfus affair was reopened, as all knew it had to be. Zola took temporary refuge in England, where he remained until 1899. When he was told that the Dreyfus case was about to be reopened, he went back to France.

During his absence dramatic events had occurred in the wake of the famous trial. Henry had broken down at a private General Staff meeting presided over by General de Boisdeffre and General Gonse and confessed that he had forged the damaging document referring to "that rogue D——." He was taken to the Mont Valérian prison under arrest, but did not wait to be tried. He committed suicide that night by cutting his throat with a razor. General de Boisdeffre resigned his post and the man who had terrorized Madame Dreyfus, Paty de Clam, was dismissed from the service.

One man at this time saw retribution too close for comfort. This was Esterhazy, for whose sake Henry had started the whole sorry scheme of subterfuge and deception. He too crossed to England. Unlike Zola, he did not return to France. Using a variety of names, he ramained in England until he died at Harpenden in 1923.

Barely two months after Henry's suicide, Madame Dreyfus formally petitioned the Cour de Cassation to allow her husband's case to be reconsidered. By this time feeling in favor of the lonely man on Devil's Island was running throughout France at full flood. When, early in 1899, the Criminal Division of the Appeal Court assented, it was time for Zola to return home. It was also time for arrangements to be made for returning Alfred Dreyfus from Devil's Island.

By this time the Dreyfus Affair was an international *cause célèbre*, and each new development of the unhurrying legal process of restoring a wronged man to his rightful place in society was followed like a gripping serial drama throughout the world.

On June 9, Dreyfus, his frame wasted by his prison life in a steaming jungle climate, walked aboard a cruiser sent to return him to France, where he arrived on the first day of the following month. He was taken to the military prison in Rennes, the capital of Brittany.

The fresh trial by court-martial opened two months later, in September, presided over by Colonel Albert Jouast. The whole of France waited for Dreyfus to be acquitted and exonerated, but the court's finding came as a shock.

At his second court-martial Alfred Dreyfus was found guilty with extenuating circumstances, whatever that was supposed to convey. The prisoner's original sentence was amended to ten years imprisonment. The Army officers comprising the court reached that decision by a majority verdict of five to two.

When the finding was published, another great outcry arose in the French Press. The Government took fright when it understood the public's anger at the mean-spirited attitude of the General Staff toward a man they could not forgive for being innocent. There were hurried consultations at the highest level, and President Loubet sought to appease his outraged countrymen by issuing a decree which was the equivalent of a "free pardon" for the bemused and unhappy Dreyfus.

To prevent further development, the Minister of War, now General de Gallifret, backed up the presidential pardon with his own order of the day, announcing that what he referred to as "the incident" was closed. He was wrong.

By this time the Government and the generals had allowed their awareness of Dreyfus the symbol to supersede sympathy for Dreyfus the man, who had yet to tell his own story. This he did in a book he entitled *Five Years of My Life*, which related the privations and sufferings he had endured on Devil's Island. He also asked why he should be pardoned for a crime he had not committed, but for which he had been severely punished.

There was no adequate answer from the Government or the Army, so the struggle to clear the pardoned man's name continued, led by Zola, who died in Paris on September 29, 1902, suffocated by fumes from a faulty chimney while he slept, only a short time before new facts came to the attention of the authorities in 1903. Even then Dreyfus was kept waiting for ultimate justice. Three years passed before, on July 12, 1906, the Cour de Cassation finally quashed the verdict of the second court-martial at Rennes.

The decision this time was unanimous.

Special measures were passed by the Government by which Dreyfus was promoted to the rank of major. He was also decorated with the Cross of Chevalier of the Legion of Honor. The same measures reappointed the stalwart Picquart, who had been dismissed, to the rank of brigadier general.

Major Dreyfus served for some months at Vincennes before retiring. On the outbreak of war in 1914 he returned to active service, was promoted to lieutenant colonel before his retirement due to age and then went to live with his family in the warmer climate of Provence. He died in Aix-en-Provence in 1935 after a year-long illness that had its roots in his privations years before on Devil's Island.

A decade later, after the close of the Second World War, the notorious and legendary penal settlement in Guiana was closed by a special commission sent from France. No single prisoner's name had done more to publicize the horrors of the fever-ridden Devil's Island, and the brutal treatment forgotten men had to undergo there, than that of Alfred Dreyfus.

The formal closure of the penal settlement was really the last act of amendment in the Dreyfus Affair, which in one way or other had been kept alive in the public mind for a full half-century.

MURDER IN HIGH SOCIETY

Six months after the Cour de Cassation finally vindicated Alfred Dreyfus and ended the series of trails and court-martials that made the Dreyfus case unique, another trial opened in New York that was to arouse world-wide interest, but for a vastly different reason.

For one thing, when the court opened, admission to the public was by ticket only, and on the morning of January 23, 1907, tickets were selling at a hundred dollars each. A hundred policemen were on duty to keep the thousands in the street outside from forcing their way bodily into the overcrowded court room, where Justice Fitzgerald presided. More than a hundred journalists and writers from America and Europe held the coveted tickets allowing them entry to cover the proceedings. Among their number were two well-known American men of Letters, Samuel Hopkins Adams and Irvin S. Cobb.

The prisoner on trail for murder was Harry Kendall Thaw, the most notorious playboy of his day in the United States, a man with a fortune of forty million dollars who had shied away from marriage until he had met lovely Evelyn Nesbit, the rather special friend of the man who was the foremost American architect of his day, Stanford White.

The person Harry Thaw was accused of murdering was this

same Stanford White. At the defense table he sat with his chief counsel, Delphin M. Delmas, a shrewd Californian who had earned the nickname of "the legal Napoleon of the Pacific Slope." He also earned the highest legal fee in America for taking a case. To get him to take the present case, the Thaw family had paid him fifty thousand dollars.

Before the trial opened, the crowded courtroom was buzzing with a rumor that the prisoner was going to plead not guilty by reason of temporary insanity. But when, shortly after the trial officially opened, a court officer called "Harry Thaw to the bar," there was a great silence, broken only by the steps of the prisoner and his chief counsel walking towards the bench where Justice Fitzgerald sat, looking stern and uncompromising.

The advancing pair made a sharp study in contrasts, for whereas Delmas was stocky and short, Thaw was much thinner, taller, and pale-faced. Both men looked suitably groomed to begin the ordeal, dressed in dark suits and trying to appear confident under the gaze of curious eyes, most of them hostile. However, when asked how the prisoner pleaded, Delmas answered in his deep voice, "We plead not guilty, if Your Honor please."

Not a word about temporary insanity.

A sigh that was like a small wind could be heard passing through the courtroom. That plea meant the trial would develop into a grim legal battle that might well become memorable, for when Stanford White had been shot, his murderer had been seen clearly by scores of witnesses holding the gun he had used.

The murder had occurred in a very public place, the roofgarden theatre of Madison Square Garden. The occasion was a notable one, the opening night of a sparkling new musical comedy with the promising name of *Mam'zelle Champagne.*

The first day of the trial was taken up with the wrangle of choosing a jury acceptable to the prosecution, led by District Attorney William Travers Jerome, and the defense, but once the jury were in their places, nine witnesses for the State of New York were promptly paraded before them to give short, terse evidence, including the physician who had extracted two bullets from the murdered man's brain, one of which had entered the left eye and the other

27

the head through the upper lip, breaking several teeth in its path. A third bullet had caused a flesh wound in Stanford White's left shoulder.

When the defense presented its case the jury were told, "Gentlemen, the defense will show that the defendant acted without malice or premeditation, and in the belief of self-defense, introduced by the threats of Stanford White to kill him."

Those words gave the clue to what was to follow. The trial was indeed to become a slanging match, and to most people seated in the New York courtroom the person who caused it, innocently or otherwise, sat with the black-garbed mother of the defendant, Mrs. William Thaw, her two daughters and son. She was Evelyn Nesbit Thaw, the wife of the man being tried for the murder of her former friend. She was dressed in very contrasting fashion to her mother-in-law. Her youthful figure was shown to advantage in a startling white shirtwaist, with a deep collar, worn under a smartly tailored blue costume. The only sombre note was the chic black velvet hat over her curls, but even this had a spray of violets at one side.

All who stared at her knew her story. For the past seven months before her husband had been brought to trial, and while he languished in New York City's Tombs Prison, feeding each day on expensive meals brought to him from the city's most fashionable restaurant, Delmonico's, that story had been featured in one form or another in newspapers throughout the United States. For Evelyn Nesbit's story had, to the average newspaper reader, read like the fairytale of Cinderella lived in a different age. The main difference between the American twentieth-century version and the story told by Perrault, a French writer of the seventeenth century, was that whereas in the original there was only one Prince Charming, in the later real-life version there were two. That proved to be one too many.

The lovely young woman seated in the New York courtroom with her gaze fixed on her husband, as though unaware that most of the spectators kept turning to stare at her, had not been born to the riches and luxury that had been showered on her. At fifteen she had all but starved to death in a squalid tenement area of New York.

She had come, with her mother and her brother, from Pennsylvania to a New York that was to be the golden city offering fame and fortune. Evelyn's mother believed that her daughter's loveliness must have a commercial value.

"You're just like a picture," she told her daughter repeatedly in the days when they had little to eat and found cash to buy food desperately hard to earn.

It was Evelyn who, fed more on her mother's enthusiasm than on substantial meals, decided she would try to get work as a model for photographers or artists. She called at agents' offices and earned little more money than it cost to repair her shoe leather and pay her bus fares. But one agent came up with a different kind of offer.

"I think I can get you in the *Floradora* chorus," he told her. "But you'll have to work hard."

"I have no objection to hard work," Evelyn told him.

She was auditioned, accepted, and worked hard. *Floradora* became a smash hit. Nightly the girl who was on her way to achieving several kinds of fame kicked her shapely legs high, tossed her head, and wriggled her bustle. She became friendly with another girl performing the same antics for a weekly wage. The new friend was Edna Goodrich, older, more sophisticated than the girl from the Pennsylvania coalfield. Edna knew her way into fashionable clubs where the men-about-town of the era had money to squander on the pleasures of the evening.

One night, after the show, she introduced Evelyn to a big man in evening dress. He had red hair and keen blue eyes that lit up when he saw Evelyn. Stanford White was an artist as well as an architect. He enjoyed female company and he had the money to indulge his tastes and preferences. For he was both rich and, in his own field, famous.

He invited Evelyn to accompany him to dinner one evening. He bought her a present to show his appreciation of his table companion. He was introduced to Mrs. Nesbit and charmed her with his easy assurance and ability to smooth over all obstacles with cash payments. Mrs. Nesbit, having met Stanford White, raised no objection to her daughter's increasing friendship with a man who earned a notice in the Society columns of New York newspapers simply by changing his favorite restaurant.

As for Evelyn, she was Cinderella with her Prince Charming,

a young woman intoxicated with life and the good things she found it could offer. She took them as a tribute to the good looks her mother had praised since she was a small child.

When Stanford White offered to give her a lavish apartment of her own where her mother could have a place, she was delighted. So the Nesbits moved. Evelyn became written up by the Society columnists. She became someone who was talked about and photographed. She had graduated from the chorus and was a star in her own right. But the stage on which she performed was a very private one, with an audience of one, Stanford White.

In Evelyn's apartment there was one special room which became the talk of the town. It had soft lights and many mirrors and a glass ceiling from which was suspended a red velvet swing, where Evelyn swung idly, dreaming away the pleasant hours, blissfully unaware of what the future held.

For her, in this halcyon period of her Cinderella life, it was enough to live for the day. She became the toast of New York. Photographs and descriptions of her featured in magazines on most newsstands in the Eastern United States. Hundreds of thousands of girls in ordinary homes looked at her picture, read about her as their daughters in another generation would read about Hollywood actresses, and envied her the good fortune that had brought her to the notice of such a man as Stanford White. One feature writer said of her:

> She is petite. Her figure is well formed and its natural curves need no artifice to accentuate them. Her hair is indeed her crowning glory—black, thick, long, and heavy. She is of the distinctly brunette type, though her eyes are deep blue, unusually large, with heavy brows arching over them. Her chin is small and, she has been told, might be a copy of the Venus de Milo's.

As for the man who had changed her life, brought her luxury and soft living and was prepared to grant her whims, there was no doubt that he was captivated by her youth and beauty and was immensely proud to feel that, in his own way, he had created the coiffured and beautifully turned-out loveliness she displayed to the hard gaze of the fashionable world. To him she was a human jewel for which he provided a fabulous setting. He thought of her as he thought of the impressive buildings he designed on paper and saw erected against the American sky. The buildings and the Evelyn Nesbit who had become the talk of New York's High Society were alike the products of his artistic genius.

He was a middle-aged man with a wife and son he saw rarely. He had a comfortable bank balance, and he used it lavishly. Evelyn could not but be impressed with the power of wealth employed by a man of taste and imagination. She had come in a very short time a long way from the days when she modelled by day and kicked up her heels in the chorus after dark. At the most, her attempt to make money on her own had brought in seventeen dollars a week from modelling with another fifteen earned in the *Floradora* chorus.

At the age of sixteen, her entire youth had been devoted to keeping her family existing just above the poverty line of those days.

As for her mother, Mrs. Nesbit's memory was in no danger of forgetting the bad times of the recent past. She could recall seeing a sheriff's officer nailing a foreclosure notice on the front door of her home, and the nights she had cried herself to sleep after trying to get employment as a dress designer.

It had been the same story when she arrived in New York and applied for work at the sweat-shops of the garment district. Now, with Evelyn installed in a lavish apartment of her own by Stanford White, the mother was looked after. She remained in the shadows left by the bright lights filling her daughter's fairytale existence, but they were comfortable shadows. She no longer went to bed at night plagued by fears for the morrow. If she had been nonplussed by the room with the red velvet swing and the mirrored walls, she found assurance in reminding herself that Stanford White was a man of taste. Moreover, he always treated her with gentle consideration.

She tried not to think of what Evelyn's life could have been like if she had found a pleasant young man and fallen in love and married him. She knew that love was a poor diet for a hungry stomach.

Taken for what it was, Evelyn's life in the years she accepted the patronage and favors of Stanford White was a period she enjoyed without thinking it could end.

That halcyon period ended when she met Harry Thaw, younger than Stanford White, richer, even more self-indulgent and vastly more cynical about most things, especially women. But like the older man, he found himself staring at Evelyn's lovely youth and suddenly he wanted her for his wife.

It seemed incredible even to himself. Harry Thaw believed himself to be genuinely in love for the first time in his life. To win her, he had to take her from Stanford White. He was confident he could, because he could offer her marriage, which was the one thing Stanford White could never bestow. Harry Thaw was a gambler who did not know what it was to lose because his resources enabled him to sit in the game long enough to emerge the winner.

He knew that what he had to offer was greater than anything Stanford White could give. He not only lived in a Pittsburgh mansion crawling with flunkies, but he had a sister married to the English Earl of Yarmouth and another whose married name was Carnegie. He himself had been for years one of the biggest social catches in America for mothers with marriageable daughters. Harry Thaw chose shrewdly the moment to enter Evelyn's life. Stanford White was engaged on a contract that demanded his full time and concentration. Evelyn, a young woman grown used to being amused by an attentive male, found Thaw's attentions flattering. She did nothing to avoid meeting him even if she did not encourage him. But Thaw was not the kind of egotist who was easily encouraged. He did only those things he wanted to do.

He stayed in Manhattan and laid siege to the most photographed girl in New York.

"Will you marry me, Evelyn?" he asked outright when he felt he was making headway.

Evelyn smiled as though she thought he was joking in poor taste.

"Come with me to Europe," he urged. "I'll show you around, and you can bring your mother as chaperone. When we get back we'll be married."

Evelyn's smile changed quality. "I'll think about it, Harry," she promised.

She did more. She talked over the new suggestion with her mother, and they both decided Harry Thaw had a reason for taking a bride-to-be to Europe. In New York the girl from Pennsylvania had acquired a veneer of culture. Europe could add to it, so that the future Mrs. Harry Thaw would be able to take her place in American Society.

The European trip was fixed up. The lush apartment with the velvet swing was vacated. Cinderella was running away from the ball. But not back to her former drudgery. She was hurrying to her second Prince Charming. Or, rather, she was hurrying across three thousand miles of ocean to keep a romantic rendezvous with him.

When she and Mrs. Nesbit arrived aboard the liner to take them to Europe, they found the finest stateroom had been reserved for them. It was a bower of superb blooms sent by Harry Thaw. He followed the woman he wanted to marry a week later.

In Paris Mrs. Nesbit proved to be an encumbrance. She was sent back to New York after visiting London. Evelyn followed her later, with a letter written by Thaw for his lawyers. She was a different young woman from the one who had sailed to Europe months earlier.

The letter she passed to Thaw's lawyers had scrawled on the outside: "Secret. Mrs. N. insisted on sailing to New York, leaving her daughter. Then her daughter left. I kept Mrs. N. in London for three months. Useless now that she has got means."

The letter in the envelope read strangely. It might have been written by a deranged person. Among other instructions was one ordering the lawyers to telephone Mrs. Nesbit and to hang up when she answered.

Stanford White had been relegated to the past. But Evelyn was not going to deny New York a chance to see her. She took a suite in the Hotel Navarre and quickly obtained a part in a stage production called *The Girl from Dixie.* When Harry Thaw belatedly arrived back in America, her pictures stared at him from the newspapers. He thrust himself back into her life. When she arrived at the Café des Beaux Arts on Sixth Avenue for dinner he was there. She told him she had been hearing stories about him. She should never believe malicious gossip, he reminded her.

Evelyn seemed aloof and more confident than she had ever been. She had returned from Europe to find New York columnists prepared to rave about her. In one journal she was labelled "The Most Beautiful Woman in the World." A story circulated that the rising young actor John Barrymore was in love with her.

If he did not wish to lose her, Harry Thaw had to stop stalling. "The Most Beautiful Woman in the World" was bathed in too much limelight. Too many admiring eyes stared at her.

He waited until Christmas Eve and then called at Evelyn's dressing-room in the Madison Square Garden Theatre. He proposed to her and was accepted, and the wedding date was fixed, and neither realized it was a curious rehearsal for another date in a grim and tragic future.

That crowded year of 1903 passed.

The wedding of Evelyn Nesbit to multimillionaire Harry Thaw was the most spectacular New York had witnessed for years. After the honeymoon Evelyn was taken by her husband to the Thaws' large estate near Pittsburgh, where for several generations the family had amassed great wealth from its coal and coke interests. There, in the house as big as a palace, with so many servants she could not remember their names, Cinderella was suddenly very lonely.

For startlingly marriage had changed Harry Thaw. He took to brooding, and the subject over which he brooded most was Stanford White, the man who had preceded him in Evelyn's affections. He became more like the person who had penned the curiously incoherent letter to his lawyers. The servants avoided him. Evelyn found she couldn't. His bad temper and demonstrations of violence became misfortunes to be endured.

But even she was startled when, not long after their first wedding anniversary, he produced a pistol and pointed it at his reflection in a mirror of his dressing-room.

Such tantrums secretly worried his mother, who felt Evelyn was to blame for the seeming change in her son. She decided to remove herself from a household where she could not be happy and in 1906 made plans for a summer visit to Europe. She went to New York, accompanied by her son and his wife, presumably to wish her *bon voyage.*

It was mid-June and New York sweltered under a heat wave. Harry Thaw's mother was glad to escape to face ocean breezes.

The heat wave reached its peak on the 25th, when Harry Thaw spent the afternoon in the lounge of the New York Whist Club. He played cards with some friends and arranged to have dinner with his wife and two other people at the Café Martin. One of these dinner companions was Truxton Beale, formerly United States Ambassador to Persia. The other was Thomas McCaleb, an author from California. Just before the Thaw party arrived at the currently fashionable restaurant, three earlier diners left. They were Stanford White, his son Lawrence, and the latter's friend and classmate at Harvard, Leroy King.

A much publicized new show, *Mam'zelle Champagne*, was opening later that night in the roof-garden theatre at Madison Square Garden. Thaw had booked seats.

However, when he arrived after dinner he found a friend seated in one he had reserved. This friend at once jumped up with an apology, bowing towards the lovely Mrs. Harry Thaw, but her husband waved a hand.

"I insist you remain," he told his friend. "I shouldn't think of disturbing you."

He turned and walked to the rear of the auditorium, where he met Stanford White's brother-in-law, James Clinch Smith, and stood chatting with him for some minutes, during which time Stanford White arrived alone.

The show was late starting. The time was ten minutes to eleven when the chorus, with fencing foils, dancing on to the stage for a number entitled *I Challenge You to a Duel*. As the number finished and the chorus danced their way off stage, the male lead came forward. Arthur Standford waited for the orchestra to cue him in, then started a number called *There was a Maid*.

From the shadows at the back of the roof-garden, feeling his way between the tables at which the audience sat, advanced a shadowy figure that stopped at a table where a tall man sat alone. Above the sound of the song a pistol shot rang out, followed by two more.

Arthur Standford stopped singing and the orchestra broke off in the middle of a bar. There was a curious silence for some moments, broken as the tall man slid from his chair to the floor. The lights came on and a number of women in the audience screamed.

On the white tablecloth on which the tall man had leaned was bright fresh blood.

Over him stood a man with a pistol in his right hand. Then the impact of the tableau was felt by the staring audience in evening dress. A millionaire had just been shot dead by another millionaire. While a light-hearted musical comedy had been running its course before the footlights, tragedy had unrolled swiftly in the shadows behind them.

Harry Thaw was seized. He offered no resistance.

"I'm glad I killed him." he declared.

The police arrived and he was taken into custody, while in the offices of New York papers perspiring men in shirt-sleeves drafted large-type headlines for the morrow's editions. One, when it appeared on the streets, read: "Pittsburgh Idler Kills Architect."

Harry Thaw was in for a bad press in the city where he had murdered a man popular with New Yorkers.

He said the wrong thing when he first came face to face with New York's District Attorney Jerome, a tough legal opponent in any courtroom.

"I saw him sitting there," he told Jerome, a sneer in his voice, "big, fat, and healthy, and there Evelyn was, poor delicate little thing, all trembling and nervous."

The District Attorney was not fooled by such hypocrisy on the part of a man who had come armed to a theatre. Expensive lawyers hurried to his aid and proclaimed him insane. When he was placed in a cell at the Thirtieth Street police station he certainly behaved like a lunatic, shouting and gesticulating and generally behaving like a man out of his mind. He was only calmed down when Bedford, his English valet, arrived with fresh clothes and linen for him and imperturbably set about the business of giving his master a new look. On the way to the police station he had objected strenuously to being handcuffed, and was told by his police escort, "We always handcuff murderers."

A hostile crowd had collected outside police headquarters at Center Street by the time he was brought there to be photographed and fingerprinted before being officially arraigned and then held on a charge of murder in the first degree. After that he was taken to the Tombs Prison to await slowly shaping events before he came to trial.

The murder became internationally famous when the liner carrying his mother to England docked and she was met by reporters anxious to give her the news and obtain her first reaction.

"My son is innocent," she stated. "If it takes the fortune of my entire family to clear him, every dollar we possess will be used to help Harry regain his freedom." It was good copy for reporters in Europe and America. So was the story that bookmakers in that citadel of Thaw wealth, Pittsburgh, were offering four to one that Harry Thaw would take his last seat in the electric chair at Sing Sing.

By the time the trial opened, Mrs. William Thaw had driven herself, her family and their lawyers relentlessly to do all they could to help her imprisoned son. To do this, Evelyn Thaw, her daughter-in-law, was subjected to a cruel examination in the courtroom.

It was all done to establish that the prisoner was justified in being homicidally jealous of the man he had seemingly supplanted in Evelyn's affections. After days of legal fire and crossfire, the battle of counsel was over. The jaded jury, who had been locked up like prisoners throughout the trial on order of Justice Fitzgerald, retired to consider their verdict.

This consideration took another three days of bickering and heated argument, by which time they still could not reach a unanimous decision. Seven voted obdurately for first-degree murder, which would have meant the death sentence, while the remaining five just as stubbornly insisted that he was guilty because he was insane.

When the jury's impasse was reported to the angry judge, he dismissed them. They had cost the taxpayers of New York a hundred thousand dollars. The Thaw family had spent five times that sum.

A second trial was ordered.

It opened nearly a year later. The same ground was trodden, the same arguments heard, the same well-dressed prisoner stared sullenly around the courtroom while most eyes turned to where his wife sat. Evelyn Thaw did not look the same as a year before. She looked much older and very tired and scared. This trial dragged on for a month. At the end of that time, the jury retired and were absent for twenty-seven hours.

It took that long to get a unanimous verdict.

"Not guilty because of insanity at the time of the act," said the foreman.

One of the most famous trials in the history of the American Bar was over. But the drama of Harry Thaw still had to run its strange zigzag course.

Because he had formally been declared insane, he vanished inside a criminal lunatic asylum. His life had been saved at fantastic cost to his family, but not his freedom.

More than six years later he escaped and managed to cross into Canada, while fresh legal exchanges, this time at international level, were made about his sanity and his freedom. He didn't wait for the outcome. He left Canada and reached New Hampshire before being arrested.

There was more legal wrangling, at the close of which he was said to be sane. In consequence he was freed, and almost his first act was to divorce his wife, who was wellnigh penniless after being repudiated by the rich family she had married into.

Harry Thaw lived for a year in the freedom of a man believed to be sane. Then his violent temper resulted in his thrashing a teenager to whom he took an intense dislike. The outcome of this uncontrolled act of violence was another hearing and his return to an asylum. This time he remained there until 1924, when he was declared to be rational and sane.

One of his first acts as a newly freed citizen was to find out what had become of his ex-wife. He learned that Evelyn was still making a living with her good looks. She was appearing in a night-club in Atlantic City.

Harry Thaw followed her, went to the night-club and sat through her performance in the floor show. When it was over he rose and left.

He was puzzled.

For minutes he had stared at the woman he had once pursued to and fro across the Atlantic, urging her to marry him, and he had not recognized her.

The lost years had turned her into a stranger.

He didn't see her again. Harry Thaw died of coronary thrombosis in Miami more than twenty years later at the age of seventy-six, no longer a Society princeling and no longer charming in any sense.

His Cinderella died quite a few years later in very reduced circumstances. For her the final threatening chimes of midnight had sounded a very long time before.

THE TRAGEDY OF OSCAR SLATER

 The tragedy of the Polish Jew born Oscar Leschziner has for more than sixty years provided a strenuous theme of argument for those who have maintained that British justice is not only far from being infallible, but that it can virtually collapse at times.

They point to the trial of Oscar Slater, as Leschziner had come to call himself, as one in which justice not only blundered, but fell flat on its dignified face. Slater was an unsavory person of dubious habits and way of living. His lack of character undoubtedly helped to convict him of a crime.

What made the conviction memorable and his trial famous was that the crime with which he was charged was murder. The trial became a classic of its kind, one where mistaken identity can wreck a man's life. There was one saving factor about the trial—it was held in Scotland before a Scots jury numbering fifteen. At the trial's close the jury took a vote. Nine of them declared he was guilty, five decided the case was not proven, which is a valid verdict under Scottish law, and the odd man out declared the prisoner was not guilty.

Under the majority vote rule valid in Scottish law at the time, this meant the prisoner was guilty. The penalty was death.

Accordingly Oscar Slater was sentenced to death.

Within hours petitions were being signed in protest at the

verdict and the sentence. Twenty thousand names appeared on one, and the petitions resulted in a great deal of publicity for the case and for the man who stood convicted of a brutal murder on evidence many thought to be highly dubious.

The crime was committed shortly before Christmas 1908, in Glasgow.

Miss Marion Gilchrist occupied what today would be called a luxury flat in Queen's Terrace in that city. She was a person of means, elderly, and employed one maid to attend to her daily requirements. Helen Lambie, the maid, had grown used to the ways of a woman of eighty-three, and life in the flat shared by the two women had settled down to a regular routine.

To some extent this was due to the fact that Miss Gilchrist, although elderly, had a will of her own. She did not like her relatives fussing over her and she did not welcome their visits. She liked to feel she was independent of them. Possibly she thought that some of them were more interested in her jewelry than in its owner. The various pieces she had acquired were worth at the time of her death something more than three thousand pounds, and they were kept locked up in the Queen's Terrace flat.

She was a Scotswoman with a strong canny streak. On the front door of the flat she had double locks, and she had a working arrangement with the family occupying the flat beneath hers. Their name was Adams. They had agreed that should they hear her knocking on the floor one of them would go up and see if she required assistance. The arrangement was comforting to the elderly spinster. It left her feeling that at no time would she be isolated, even when Helen Lambie was away from the flat.

The maid was in the habit of leaving the flat most evenings to get her mistress an evening paper. Usually this meant a short walk to a nearby shop. The journey to and from the newsstand took about ten minutes.

On the evening of December 21, 1908, Helen Lambie donned her hat and coat and told her mistress she was going out to get the paper. It was just about seven o'clock when she left the flat and started down Queen's Terrace. She had not been gone longer than the customary ten minutes when she returned to the flats, climbed to Miss Gilchrist's front door, and pulled up in surprise at the sight of Mr. Adams from the flat below trying to peer through a keyhole.

"Why, Mr. Adams," she said, "what's the matter?"

The man straightened and turned a worried-looking face to the maid.

"Oh, I'm glad you've come back," he said. "I heard some strange and rather loud noises coming from overhead and thought I'd better see if Miss Gilchrist is all right."

Helen Lambie produced her keys.

"We'll soon see," she said, fitting one of her keys in the first lock.

After unlocking the door she stepped into the hall beyond with Mr. Adams close behind.

"I expect it was only the pulleys in the kitchen," she turned to say, and as she did so a man who was a stranger darted past both the maid and Mr. Adams and ran down to the street.

He was in too much of a hurry to look where he was going in the poorly lit street and collided with a girl on the pavement. The girl cried out, and almost fell. The man took no notice and did not turn to help her recover her balance. He sped into the night.

Meantime Helen Lambie had gone into the kitchen of the flat to inspect the pulleys attached to the ceiling. They were as she remembered leaving them. She next went to Miss Gilchrist's bedroom, which was deserted.

Behind her Mr. Adams said anxiously, "Where is your mistress? Is she in the flat?" Helen Lambie, suddenly feeling very anxious, turned and made her way into the dining room. There they found Miss Gilchrist. The white-haired woman had been bludgeoned over the head and her wrinkled face was a bright mask of blood. There was a pool of blood near the body lying on the floor and blood on the furniture.

A rug had been dropped across her body.

"That man!" cried the maid.

Mr. Adams, appalled by the sight in the dining room, turned and ran in pursuit of the stranger who had fled from the flat. Not surprisingly, by the time he reached Queen's Terrace and stood staring up and down the street, the mysterious man who had run from the flat had vanished in the December night. The nonplussed neighbor of the dead woman turned up his collar against the chill and set out to get a doctor and to inform the police of what had happened.

The doctor he summoned had the same name as himself, but shortly after he arrived at the flat and examined the pathetic corpse in the dining room, the police came with their own surgeon, who took over from Dr. Adams, so that the latter was never called to give evidence at the trial.

Two things seemed fairly obvious to the investigating Scots police. The man who had escaped in such a panicky way from the flat could tell them what had happened in the dining room during the time Helen Lambie had gone to buy an evening paper. Also, motive for the crime was a very simple one. Robbery.

An ornamental wooden box that had contained the dead woman's private papers lay broken in her dressing room. Pieces of jewelry were scattered in disorder, as though someone had rummaged through them in a hurry.

However, when a check was made with Helen Lambie, only one piece was missing. A valuable brooch comprising a cluster of good quality diamonds.

It was some time later that a Mrs. Barrowman went to her front door to let in her fifteen-year-old daughter Mary. The girl was late, and her mother was on the point of scolding her when the girl began an excitedly told story of how a man had rushed from a house in Queen's Terrace, nearly knocking her down, and then disappeared into the night.

Mrs. Barrowman shut the front door and followed her daughter into the family living room.

"You'd better have your supper and get to bed, Mary," she said, "and don't make up stories."

But the next day Mrs. Barrowman read of the murder in a Queen's Terrace flat and changed her mind about Mary's story. She told the police and was visited by a detective, to whom she said, "Our Mary can describe this man who ran away up Queen's Terrace."

The girl was questioned, and her description of the man who had charged into her was taken down. It appeared to the detectives on the case to vary in certain particulars from the description already given them by Helen Lambie. Accordingly they played safe and circulated both to the English and Scottish press. Their description of the missing brooch was more positive.

The Glasgow and London newspapers gave the murder inquiry full coverage. Within hours after publication of the police descriptions, a bicycle dealer named Allan McLean called at a police station with information. He explained that he was a member of a social organization called the Sloper Club.

"We've got a member we call Oscar," he told the police. "He's been trying to get rid of a diamond brooch."

He added that this Oscar was a German Jew with a sallow complexion and moustache, was stockily built, usually wore a bowler hat and carried a walking stick, and lived in a house not far from Queen's Terrace, though he did not know the precise address.

"Can you take us to the house?" the police asked McLean.

"Yes," said the bicycle dealer.

They accompanied him to another building rented as flats, where they were both surprised and encouraged to learn that the man known as Oscar had moved out on Christmas Day. With him had gone a woman who lived at the same address. The police were met by a maid who told them she had no idea where the couple had gone.

While waiting to find the whereabouts of the man who had intriguingly started his travels on the one day in the year when most people remain by a fireside, the police began inquiries about the brooch that had been offered for sale, according to McLean. They obtained a description of the piece of jewelry.

It did not fit the description of Marion Gilchrist's missing diamond brooch.

But while trying to learn of the missing Oscar's whereabouts, the Glasgow police filled in quite a number of what seemed significant details about the man's background. He was using the name Oscar Slater. He was not of British birth. He was a man who had already been known by several names, one of which he had used when he married, although he was separated from his wife. He had informed acquaintances that he was a dentist, but the enquiring police could not learn of any occasion when he had acted as one. On the other hand, he had frequently appeared with pieces of jewelry for sale.

Oscar Slater sounded like an unsavory person. The police continued their checking.

They found that he had booked a passage to the United States and had sailed four days after the murder of Miss Gilchrist. At first glance, that looked very much like flight. It was in keeping with the desperate dash into the street of the man who had run from the hall of the flat in Queen's Terrace and almost knocked down Mary Barrowman.

The police began to fill in gaps in what they considered a pattern of events. They spoke to a ticket agent at the railway station nearest to Queen's Terrace. He told them that some time after seven o'clock on the night of the murder, he had sold a ticket to a passenger who was so agitated and trembling that he made no attempt to collect it, but had hurried away with his head tucked down.

Alongside this they set the story of a tram conductor who mentioned the murder to a passenger who had just bought a ticket. The man had at once got up and left the tram.

A number of females, obviously impressed by the drama of the occasion, assured the detectives who talked to them that they had seen a man standing in Queen's Terrace eyeing the flat in which the murder had been committed. Loosely the description of this man fitted that of a shadowy Oscar Slater, who was being sought by the New York police after a request received from Glasgow. Extradition proceedings were completed after the man who had left Glasgow that Christmas was arrested in New York. Helen Lambie, with an excited Mary Barrowman having the time of her life, arrived in New York and was taken to see the man under arrest. Short, scared Oscar Slater was brought to them by a deputy marshal well over six feet in height who dwarfed the man considered to be a fugitive from the law.

"That's the man," declared the two females from Scotland who had once, quite a few days before, caught a glimpse of a man who had kept his face averted while he ran from them.

Oscar Slater did not fight the extradition warrant that had been issued. He returned to Britain, a man who was convinced he could make the Scots police realize a mistake had been made. When he stepped off the ship he was met by waiting police. His luggage was searched. It contained two items the police considered self-evident as involving the man in custody. One was a stained macintosh. Certain stains on it looked like blood. The other was a hammer that weighed half a pound. It had no stains that could be considered gruesome.

Slater made a statement.

He explained that he had arranged to go to America several weeks before he sailed. He had used a false name in which to book his passage because he didn't want his wife to know he had left the country. The reason he had not gone until Christmas was that he had been waiting to let his flat.

To the police it sounded plausible at best, but as an explanation in a murder case they deemed it unsatisfactory. To them the departure still looked like flight in a panic to avoid arrest. Moreover, they now had evidence that Slater had actually pawned a diamond brooch he hadn't been able to sell. Obviously, between December 21 when the murder was committed, and four days later when Oscar Slater had sailed for the New World and presumably a hopeful new life, he had been in sudden need of funds. That too looked damaging, when considered with all the other scraps of poorly fitting pieces in the pattern they had created. But viewed from a distance the pattern looked impressive. The loose fit of the individual pieces comprising it then became blurred.

Every police inquiry was directed to making Oscar Slater fit the role of Miss Gilchrist's callous and brutal slayer. No independent inquiry was begun to find an alternative to the bemused little Jew babbling unsatisfactory explanations about his highly suspicious movements.

He was charged with the murder committed at 15 Queen's Terrace, and the chief witnesses for the prosecution were the two young females—the dead woman's maid, who was twenty-one, and the fifteen-year-old Mary Barrowman—and the man who had been concerned whether his ceiling would crack when Miss Gilchrist's body dropped to the dining-room floor, Arthur Adams.

The trial opened in May 1909, in the High Court of Justiciary in Edinburgh before Lord Guthrie. Many times since that notable hearing closed, the proceedings have been criticized. For one thing, although the defense reminded the jury of a miscarriage of justice in the notorious case of Adolf Beck, it did not go out of its way to challenge a vindictive attack by the Lord Advocate, Mr. Alexander Ure, K.C., that was not in line with the relevant evidence in the case. The Lord Advocate went out of his way to attack the prisoner for his character, as pictured by the Glasgow police. After censuring Slater for the immoral and shiftless life he had led, the resounding voice of the leader of the prosecution declared: "I say without hesitation that the man in the dock is capable of having committed this dastardly outrage."

The defense should have been on its feet, protesting. It remained seated.

Alexander Ure was out to get a conviction. Perhaps he appeared to have blood in his eye. He was certainly an intimidating figure when he got into his haranguing stride. He indulged in an exercise of raw prejudice in order to influence the fifteen grim faces over the rail of the jury box. He told them that Slater was a man who had lived, as he chose to phrase it, "a life which descends to the very lowest depths of human degradation."

He was even able to top that piece of gratuitous information.

"Slater," he told them, "probably is the worst of men."

That was a day when the scales of Justice were heard to clink. Someone was adjusting the weights and impartiality was forgotten. Slater was presented as though he were worthy of being hangman's bait.

It is this aspect of the trial that today makes it seem a blot on the pages of British courtroom history. The man in the dock had almost no hope of beating the evidence offered by the prosecution. It was not sound evidence. It was evidence based on certain misbeliefs and possibly on emotion, for it amounted to no more than positive identification by persons who were in no position to be positive.

The three witnesses on whose evidence rested the case for the prosecution all went into the witness box, and each of them swore on oath that the man they had seen hurrying from the Gilchrist flat closely resembled Oscar Slater. Arthur Adams was actually very nearsighted, and the Barrowman girl admitted that she was shown photographs of the prisoner before she went to New York to identify him. Moreover, Helen Lambie had only seen the hurrying man in profile. To the best of her recollection he was clean-shaven. Yet Oscar Slater wore a moustache and had also worn one on the day of the murder.

Despite the three chief prosecution witnesses having earlier given different accounts of the hurrying man's appearance, by the time they appeared in Edinburgh they had more or less eradicated those differences. A strong defense could have shaken them like poorly rooted trees in a gale. The defense of Oscar Slater was neither strong nor aggressive.

The jury was led to believe that the clean hammer found in Slater's baggage had accompanied him to America aboard the *Lusitania* when he sailed for a refuge three thousand miles distant. But the experts summoned to bolster the prosecution's case were cautious. More than fifty vicious and fast blows had shattered Marion Gilchrist's head according to the medical evidence. Could Slater's hammer have been the weapon?

Professor Glaister considered that it could, but admitted that he could not positively declare it had been. The opinions of three medical men varied. Dr. Veitch was of the opinion that the hammer taken from Slater's baggage was too light to be the weapon used. In his view the actual weapon had been much heavier. Dr. Robertson agreed with this. On the other hand, Dr. Galt tended to side with the professor. He thought the hammer could have been the weapon used, but hedged by admitting that he had earlier expected the weapon to have been heavier.

None of this was helpful to the Scots jury, who had to listen to the often pointless remarks of a vast parade of witnesses, no less than sixty summoned by the prosecution. Against this array of overt partisanship, the defense produced fourteen who offered some sort of testimony allegedly on behalf of the glum-looking prisoner.

He had every right to look glum.

When Slater talked over the case with his counsel, he said he wanted to give evidence. He felt that if he went into the witness box and told his own story he would be believed. His counsel decided this would be a tactical error. Possibly the defense understood that too many people had no wish to believe the man who was accused of such a frightful slaughter. Whatever the reason, the arguments of the defending counsel prevailed. Oscar Slater did not give evidence on his own behalf.

More than sixty years later it is easy to see the omission as a blunder, but today one is viewing events with a detachment afforded by the sharp perspective of more than half a century. Just possibly the Scots defense believed that the uncertain aspects of the identification testimony would mean that the jury would decide there remained a strong reasonable doubt.

If such was indeed the case the defense was guilty of not assessing correctly the quality of the judge hearing the case. Lord Guthrie was a strong-minded man, but he could hardly be termed a fair-minded one during those May days in 1909 when he sat listening to the evidence in the trial of Oscar Slater.

When the time came for him to be helpful and sum up for the jury, he went out of his way to attack the prisoner's character. It has been pointed out that as Slater had not pleaded good character in his defense, his character should not have been called in question, as a matter of law, by either the prosecuting counsel or the judge. But Lord Guthrie seemed to side with the Lord Advocate. He told the jury the prisoner had been living a lie.

"Not only a lie for years, but is so today," he declared in his deep impressive tones. He went on to assure the listening jury that Slater had lived "in a way that many blackguards would scorn to do," and he informed them that the prisoner "has not the presumption of innocence in his favor, which is a form in the case of every man, but a reality in the case of the ordinary man."

It was neither good law nor good philosophy, for this bald reference to the prisoner's guilt by denying his innocence was to have repercussions nearly twenty years later.

When at last the majority verdict was brought in, Slater was impelled to lean forward to shout at the group of fifteen jurymen who looked anything but pleased with themselves: "I know nothing about the affair. You are convicting an innocent man!"

A move was made to quell the outburst. It had not made the jury look any happier.

Lord Guthrie certainly did not look moved by it.

Very deliberately he took his time sentencing the unhappy man who had been hurriedly silenced the only time he had spoken impulsively on his own behalf during the trial.

Oscar Slater heard himself condemned to be hanged.

The date was fixed for May 27.

But in the interim between the trial's end and the day the condemned man was due to receive a visit from the public hangman, those protests and petitions with thousands of names were issued. The Jew with the unprepossessing manner who had tried to sell a brooch in the Glasgow Sloper Club and had actually pawned one on November 18, three weeks before the murder of which he had been convicted, was suddenly seen in a broadly national perspective as a pathetic figure who had received less than justice in a British court.

The outcry was heard in Scotland and south of the border, and some of the persons whose voices were heard were in that decade people of consequence, notably Sir Arthur Conan Doyle. Before the gallows could be built, Slater heard that he had been granted a reprieve from the death sentence, which had been commuted to imprisonment for life.

Still claiming he was innocent of Miss Gilchrist's murder, he vanished inside a prison's walls. But he was not forgotten. Others joined with the redoubtable creator of Sherlock Holmes to demand that justice be accorded the convicted murderer. There were questions in the House of Commons, but no reason was given publicly for the reprieve.

It was not good enough.

Sir Edward Marshall-Hall added his voice to Conan Doyle's in a demand for justice for Oscar Slater. Lord Buckmaster echoed the demand. So did Edgar Wallace. One newspaper, the *News Chronicle,* made it a matter of policy to set out the facts of the case periodically in the years to follow, always in the hope that the authorities would relent.

As time passed the volume of demand grew. The constant airing of considered opinions about the unfairness of the Edinburgh trial began to make an impression on the thick skin of reluctant authority. Writers and publicists who were deeply concerned about the unsatisfactory outcome of Slater's arrest began preparing new theories. They reverted to one of the first theories of the Glasgow police, that two men had been concerned with the murder and robbery, to explain the crowded events of a mere ten minutes.

Eventually that demand for a fresh hearing of the case fell on ears that were not deaf to the arguments of mercy and reason. It was arranged for a formal appeal to be heard in that same court in Edinburgh where Oscar Slater had been condemned in a manner that made him a martyr to many.

The second appearance of Oscar Slater in that court was made nineteen years after the first. He was a different man, one who had spent more than eighteen years in jail, years that had changed him inwardly and outwardly. He took his place in the courtroom and stared around him resentfully. He was not a man grateful for the work of many who had afforded him this second chance. He was a man with a weighty chip on his shoulder. He felt wronged, and was in no mind to let anyone forget it.

The appeal, as everyone knew it would, went in his favor. He was formally released. Afterwards, another formality pardoned him for that crime of which he had always said he was innocent. Then arose the question of compensation.

He was given six thousand pounds.

It was a sizable sum, but it did not change his resentment, and curiously this expressed itself most keenly in the manner in which he showed his dislike for Conan Doyle, who had done more than any person to wake up the authorities to their obligations to a misjudged man.

So keenly did he resent Conan Doyle's interest that he refused to express any gratitude towards anyone who had worked with the author to jog the public conscience. That resentment on Slater's part is not the least of the many anomalies with which his story teems.

However, Justice had belatedly been served and, moreover, been seen to be served, and Oscar Slater was no longer a subject to make men uncomfortable in their thoughts. Oscar Slater merged into the Scots mists into which he had been released.

A little more than a decade after being granted his freedom and a "free pardon," he married, in 1937, nearly thirty years after standing trial for murder. He and his wife went to live in Ayr. The man who had lived throughout the First World War in prison lived through the Second in his own home.

But he did not long survive the end of hostilities. He died in 1948, in his seventy-fifth year, a man remembered neither for his vices nor his virtues, but only for the notable miscarriage of justice in which he featured as the unfortunate principal.

THE ORIGINAL WINSLOW BOY

In 1910 a boy of thirteen, a cadet at the Royal Naval College at Osborne, on the Isle of Wight, became the focus of a great deal of attention. His name was George Archer-Shee, and he arrived at the college in every expectation of spending his life in a naval career. However, he was fated to die wearing the uniform of a different Service.

The chief reason was a postal money order for five shillings. The money order was said to have been stolen, and George Archer-Shee had been branded as the thief after some witnesses who were much too sure of themselves had given some very cloudy testimony.

The fight to clear the lad's name and to make the Lords of the Admiralty accept their responsibilities in a tragic case of injustice created such a scandal that it took Sir Edward Carson, the great advocate of the first year of the present century, two years to have it put right.

By that time there was no question of young Archer-Shee returning to a Service that had, in its own terminology, cast him adrift.

The affair opened for the shocked family of the cadet when in 1908 his father, Martin Archer-Shee, received an unusual request by mail from the Lords Commissioners of the Admiralty. In excessively cool terms the father was requested to remove his son from the Royal Naval College. The explanation was brief and succinct. It had been reported that a money order had been stolen from another cadet a short while before, and Mr. Archer-Shee was bluntly informed that "investigation leaves no other conclusion possible than that it was taken by your son."

Martin Archer-Shee was incensed by the request and the terms in which it was couched. He composed a formal reply to the Admiralty, in which he asserted that he would never accept that his son was a thief. He said nothing about removing his son from Osborne.

Instead, he and his elder son, Major Martin Archer-Shee, who was a Member of Parliament, set out to catch the ferry to the Isle of Wight. They arrived to find themselves confronted by men with their minds made up. The college heads were convinced that young George had stolen the money order from a cadet named Terence Back, and they were not prepared to listen to pleas or arguments.

"We must ask you to remove your son, Mr. Archer-Shee," George's father was told.

The heavy-hearted father agreed, making a great effort to keep his temper. George was instructed to pack his things, and a glum trio returned to London. On the journey, George's father and step-brother discussed what should be done. There was no question of their doubting the lad's claim that he was innocent of the charge. He had said he didn't steal the money order and that was good enough for his father and step-brother. They believed they knew the boy better than his instructors at the Royal Naval College.

Equally there was no question of what was to be done. The young cadet's expulsion from Osborne had to be fought. In that way his name would be cleared. Moreover, it could only be cleared in the courts.

By the time the Archer-Shee trio had reached London, the elder son had convinced his father where he should go for the best advice in the unusual circumstances.

"Sir Edward Carson will give us the best advice, father. If we can get him to take the case we can confidently leave things in his hands. There's no better advocate in the country."

The younger Martin Archer-Shee had no difficulty in persuading the elder to agree, for George's father realized that a die had been cast when George was expelled from Osborne. The Lords of the Admiralty would be unwilling to lose face. They would support the action taken by the Osborne authorities. The real business for any advocate who undertook to clear George's name at a formal hearing was to bring the Admiralty to agree to a hearing within the law. They might very easily adopt the lofty attitude that they were above it.

Sir Edward Carson was approached. He agreed to see the boy for himself.

"Bring him to see me," he told the older Archer-Shee. "In his uniform," he added, a request that surprised his listeners.

Young George was taken to see the famous advocate, and he arrived in his Osborne uniform, the sight of which made Carson's eyes crinkle slightly at the corners. It was a familiar uniform to him.

His own son wore it.

Carson was an impressive man in court. He was no less impressive in the surroundings of his barrister's chambers. Young George found himself answering questions that were designed to test him and to discover if he would prevaricate or attempt to be hypocritical.

It was at this interview in Carson's chambers that the first real story of what had happened was told in sequence by the youngster who had been branded a thief. He told Carson how at breakfast one day a fellow cadet named Back had said he had received in the morning's post a postal money order for five shillings. Terence Back and George Archer-Shee were friends. George was with Terence when the latter put his newly received money order in his writing-case, which he took to his locker.

At tea time the same day Terence Back went to his locker and found the door had been forced open. When he opened his writing-case, the money order for five shillings was not inside. He turned away from his rifled locker and reported what had happened. Immediate inquiries were made, and the chief petty officer reported that on the afternoon when the theft was discovered only two cadets from the college had been given formal leave to go to the nearby village post office. One of the names on his record sheet was Cadet Archer-Shee.

The post office received a visit, and after answering questions put to her, the postmistress agreed to call at the college on the following morning to be interviewed by Commander Colton. At that interview she told the frowning officer that, on the afternoon of the locker theft, two cadets had called at the post office and purchased postal money orders. She recalled that one had given his name as Arbuthnot. The second, she said, had bought a money order for fifteen shillings and sixpence. However, this second cadet had also cashed a money order.

It was for five shillings.

She had asked him to write his name on the endorsement line, and he had written "Terence H. Back."

Commander Colton knew that the boy who had bought the postal order for fifteen and six was Archer-Shee. The cadet had told him quite candidly. The boy had wanted the money order to pay for a model engine he wished to buy. The commander decided to hold an identity parade, and his visitor was asked to pick out from the line of cadets the two who had called at her counter and bought money orders.

The flustered woman, unaware of what was involved and feeling very uncomfortable in surroundings she found rather forbidding, walked down the line of cadets paraded for her scrutiny. When she came to the end of the line she had not recognized either of the two cadets. The identity parade had proved nothing except that the postmistress had a poor memory for faces. To her all the youngsters in similar dark blue uniforms with shiny buttons and standing with the same stance appeared practically indistinguishable from one another.

"I'm sorry," she said miserably. "I can't recognize them."

The ball had been returned to Commander Colton, and he played it vigorously. He sent for the boy under a cloud and told him to write the name of his friend Back. George sat down and across a fresh piece of paper wrote in a slanting hand, "Terence H. Back".

Commander Colton now had this signature, together with the postal money order he had recovered, sent to Mr. Guerrin, who had already made a grave error of judgement as a handwriting expert in another famous case. Mr. Guerrin was no less positive in the case of young George Archer-Shee. After comparing the signatures on the sheet of paper and on the endorsement line of the postal order, he declared that both had been written by the same person.

Again Commander Colton had to play the ball which had bounced back to him. He summoned the cadet whom he now believed to be a thief and a liar and told him of the handwriting expert's verdict on the signatures.

"I am innocent, I swear it," said the flushed and very scared boy, staring wide-eyed at the grave-faced man in front of him.

Possibly just for a moment Commander Colton had a doubt. He knew that young Archer-Shee was far from being among the brightest of his brood, but he had always appealed to his superiors as honest and likeable for his personal qualities. This act was totally out of character.

But if such a doubt was entertained, the commander was easily able to resolve it. Circumstances, as he saw them, were damning. It was true that he had also learned that Archer-Shee's own locker had been forced open the same afternoon, but that could merely point to cunning calculated to deceive. On the other hand Archer-Shee was not short of cash at the time of the theft. He had a bank credit of more than six pounds. But having money did not mean a boy would not take more for himself.

However, Percy Scholes was a different matter.

This cadet had not been in the post office on the afternoon when the money order was cashed, but he had seen Archer-Shee leave it shortly after two o'clock, and had said so when questioned. Against this, the postmistress had said she thought it was about three o'clock when she paid out five shillings for the postal order endorsed in the name of "Terence H. Back."

It was not unknown for people to be mistaken about time. But in the case of Cadet Scholes the chances were slim. It took a bare five minutes to walk from the college to the village post office, and he was positive Archer-Shee had walked out of the college grounds and started down the road to the village only a few minutes after two. So, in Commander Colton's view, the postmistress had been mistaken.

But Mr. Guerrin was a rock he could depend on.

He dismissed the unhappy warm-faced boy in his office and drafted the letter to the lad's father.

This was the story Sir Edward Carson went over with young

George in an interview made dramatic by Terence Rattigan in his dramatization of the Archer-Shee story in his well-known play *The Winslow Boy.*

Carson was in his time without peer as an advocate. He trusted his judgement of people, and once he had agreed to defend a person charged with a crime he spared neither himself nor the person he was defending. He was essentially a wholehearted barrister, as his chief clerk, overburdened with work in the busiest suite of chambers in the Temple, could have attested. And he was a whole-hearted fighter. When he took a case he went into court not for the purpose of earning his substantial fee, but to win for his client.

Such a man was a tough opponent, as the lords of the Admiralty were to discover after Carson had been satisfied by the answers young George Archer-Shee had given to his own searching questions.

Having made the case of clearing George's name his own, the redoubtable Irish advocate lost no time in firing the opening shots to test the range.

He began by trying to manoeuvre the Admiralty into agreeing to hold a judicial inquiry into the case, but it was time wasted except to confirm his opinion of the temper of the opposition. A formal investigation was belatedly opened by a Judge Advocate of the Fleet, but only when the outcome was not in doubt. The Osborne College inquiry was elevated to a more imposing status, with the same evidence considered.

Carson was not put out of stride by this expected rebuff intended to make the Admiralty's challengers lose heart. The case was complicated, he knew, because his client was too young to be a midshipman, which is a commissioned rank allowing the right to demand a court-martial in such an instance. A mere cadet, being only a schoolboy with special naval training, had no such right.

There was one opening, and Carson tried it. He could bring the Admiralty to court if a criminal prosecution against them were started. But that meant getting the co-operation of the Director of Public Prosecutions, and that gentleman was not disposed to throw down a challenge to the powerful Lords of the Admiralty simply on the unsupported word of a boy who had been charged with stealing five shillings. Carson was as good as told not to lose his sense of proportion.

The stubborn Irishman required no such advice, especially as months had passed before he received it. Indeed, a whole year went by with Carson no further ahead than on the day he had said he would accept the Archer-Shee case. He decided on a change of tactics.

"We'll try what we can do by petition of right," he told George's discouraged but still resolute father. "That may get them out of their seats."

"But if they won't assent to the hearing?" Martin Archer-Shee asked.

"Then," Carson smiled grimly, "there is no action. But we can serve notice we're still at battle stations."

The intention was to bring an action against the Admiralty for breach of contract by refusing to complete the naval training of the dismissed cadet. The Admiralty bided its time, until Carson appeared before Mr. Justice Ridley on July 12, 1910 to present his case. In the same courtroom the Solicitor General offered strong legal objection to the proceedings being held, claiming that no contract had been entered into between the Admiralty and Cadet Archer-Shee. The Admiralty reserved the right to dismiss a cadet as it would dismiss a naval officer.

Carson's move had been blocked.

But the case was really out in the open for the first time, and Carson made the most of an occasion that he knew would be reported and given wide publicity. The formidable advocate did not have to simulate the indignation he felt.

He pointed out that a department of State had used its prerogative to take away a boy's good name without giving him any chance to defend it.

"This," he said in a resounding voice, "amounts to a public scandal. The Crown can be high-handed out of court, but in open court it isn't to be tolerated."

Mr. Justice Ridley was sympathetic, and in an effort to be conciliatory to the opposed sides suggested that the facts be given an airing.

However, the Solicitor General stood pat. He had his instructions from the Admiralty and they were not to budge from his legal position.

He insisted that this consideration of the facts of the case was unnecessary because he was entitled in law to judgement. Carson appealed to the judge, pointing out the lengthy period for which he had been endeavoring to obtain a hearing of the case at which the defendant could give evidence on his own behalf.

This time, he found, Mr. Justice Ridley was unable to help him, despite his sympathy. The objection to the hearing raised by the Solicitor General was an objection valid in law. The judge had to agree with the Solicitor General as spokesman for the Admiralty.

Carson came close to losing his Irish temper.

"This is a case of the grossest oppression without remedy," he declared, "that I have known since I have been at the Bar."

The Solicitor General, who was Rufus Isaacs, later to be Lord Reading, refused to have his legal armor dented by such a fulsome declaration. He knew Carson had been defeated on a legal technicality and was content to wait until his opponent left the field. Before walking out, Carson had a last comment, which he hurled dead on target.

"This is a gross outrage by the Admiralty," he said savagely.

All he had left to support him as he strode from the court was his determination in some way to force the Admiralty's hand, come what may. That day he became not only a determined advocate. He was a dedicated defender.

The publicity the case received after the Solicitor General had blocked Carson's latest efforts was encouraging. He appealed against Mr. Justice Ridley's ruling, and within a week Lord Justice Vaughan-Williams was asking for the facts, and when the Solicitor General objected to having them provided on legal grounds, he heard himself overruled.

He saw amply demonstrated Carson's determination to be ready to seize any advantage offered. No sooner had the appeal court ruled that the case should be heard by a judge and jury than Carson was delivering an application for a speedy trial to the Lord Chief Justice.

Carson could perceive eventual victory, and wanted no further time wasted in maneuvering and countermaneuvering. Young

George Archer-Shee was two years older than when he had been forced to leave Osborne. These were the important formative years of his life that were being wasted by delayed action in the courts.

It was July 1910 when the case of the boy the Admiralty had dismissed as a thief and a liar was finally heard before a British jury in a crowded courtroom. It was only a short time before the courts closed for the Long Vacation, but Carson, overtired from too many demands made on his time, appeared and opened his case with a show of resilience and fervor that amazed even friends who had known him for many years and well understood his qualities and capacities. He was determined to make the headlines.

"The suppliant father," he stated, "asks for his son only that which every street arab obtains. Indeed, he does not ask for so much. The street arab has the protection of a trained magistrate, of a jury presided over by a judge, and of the Court of Criminal Appeal."

Then he began his denunciation.

"The Admiralty," he went on, "having taken a position, will naturally never go back. They have fought and they will fight to the bitter end. I suppose a department has no heart and does not understand a father's broken heart."

Carson was speaking to a jury which, ironically, was never called upon to give its verdict. He was still speaking to the attentive faces in the jury box when he continued, "I will not trouble you with the technical legal defenses in this case. I will put the boy before you on the plain issue—is he a thief and forger or is he not?"

However, he ran into trouble when he told the jury that he might be taking the opportunity of questioning the handwriting expert, Mr. Guerrin, about his evidence given in previous cases. That was a plain reference to the Adolf Beck case, and the judge told him, "That observation is unworthy of you, Sir Edward. Everybody knows Mr. Guerrin."

Carson resented the judge's remark, but the judge refused to withdraw it.

In such an atmosphere the jury were kept on the edges of their uncomfortable seats.

Carson went on to explain that Commander Colton had seemed surprised that George had known how Terence Back signed his name, but pointed out that the surprising thing would have been if he hadn't. The boys slept in beds next to each other, were close friends, and had often been in one another's company from getting up in the morning till going to bed at night.

Once in his stride, Carson made the most of his opportunity. He had waited a long while to censure the Admiralty and he took this chance to deliver a bitter reproach. Indeed, the judge felt he had to object.

Carson was sensitive to disapproval from the Bench, and was quick to protest, "You are censuring me, my Lord, in what you supposed I was saying."

The judge returned rather grimly, "And you are censuring everyone, and I suppose it's my turn now."

An awkward moment had been turned into one of the case's lighter ones by the judge's shrewd riposte. Carson saw grins on the faces nearest him.

He put Martin Archer-Shee in the witness box and drew from the father a telling assessment of his son's character. He was not shaken by cross-examination from the Solicitor General. When young George followed his father into the box he was not in for the shattering session for which he had been prepared. When the Solicitor General found he could not shake the boy's story or his assertion of his innocence he gave up. It was too much like being the devil's advocate, and the round-faced boy with the wide clear eyes could too easily be made to look to the jury like a martyr going to the stake for his faith. When Terence Back appeared for the Admiralty he rather dented their case by saying Archer-Shee knew how he signed his name just as he knew how Archer-Shee signed his. The postmistress was a stumbling block, for she genuinely believed the testimony she had already given, but Cadet Scholes demolished the time obstacle by explaining how Archer-Shee had asked him to go with him to the post office to cash a money order. He was expecting friends and could not leave the college. That was at quarter past two.

The Solicitor General asked how he could be so sure of the time.

"Because," said the cadet, "I kept looking at the clock to see if my friends were due."

Arbuthnot, the other cadet with permission to go to the post office, neither added to nor detracted from the general weight of evidence, but a telegraph boy who had been questioned was now produced to swear that he had seen a cadet enter the post office at ten past two, while a second entered and left about half-past.

However, it was the chief petty officer who had first received news of the theft from Cadet Back's locker who unintentionally shifted the hitherto firmly grounded case the Admiralty had put forward. He not only differed from the postmistress in a number of relevant details as to what was said, but the information was elicited from him that there had been similar thefts from the locker room at Osborne College.

Some had been before young George had been dismissed. But, very significantly, there had been others that had occurred since his leaving.

At that the jury began to stir restively. The judge became closely attentive of the notes he had been making.

The day's hearing closed with a wrangle about the Judge-Advocate of the Fleet giving evidence because, as Carson pointed out, his original inquiry had been made without George Archer-Shee being present. That began the wrangle, with the judge trying to squash Carson by citing instances of claims about law officers' rights.

"I can give instances," he said.

"They are getting out of date," Carson retorted.

Possibly it was just as well for everyone's blood pressure that the hearing did not continue until the last testimony had been given and the final witness heard.

The morning brought a very considerable change in the proceedings, for overnight there had been some hard thinking by the Lords of the Admiralty, at last aware that they were being made to appear in a very unfavorable light to the British public.

After the court had assembled Rufus Isaacs rose and made a speech that was virtually an apology to a wronged cadet.

He said: "As to the issues of fact, the court and jury will not be further troubled. I say now, on behalf of the Admiralty, that I accept the declaration of George Archer-Shee that he did not write the name on the postal order, that he did not take it, and that he did not cash it—and that consequently he was innocent of the charge that was brought against him."

While the jury and others in the courtroom were catching their breath after this about-face in a hurry, the Solicitor General continued: "I make that statement without any reservation of any description, intending it to be a complete acceptance of the boy's statements."

When Rufus Isaacs finished, every head was turned to look at the man who had fought to make victory possible. Edward Carson could not hide the tears in his eyes. When he rose he spoke huskily with deep-felt emotion, and he told the court: "The vindication of George Archer-Shee was the object of this action. It has been entirely achieved."

That was the signal for the jury to leave their box and crowd around him to shake his hand. Rufus Isaacs stood by, smiling an enigmatic smile at the outcome of his announcement. It had fore-stalled a smarting defeat, for it was plain at that moment where the sympathies of the jury lay.

They could not congratulate young George, however, because he was not in court. He had been taken to the theatre the previous evening, and had overslept.

When the happy Carson was told this by George himself, the man who had cleared George's name showed surprise.

"Weren't you too nervous about the outcome," he asked, "to think of going to the theatre?"

George gave him that clear-eyed look that had won the jury to his cause.

"I didn't have the slightest nervousness," the lad said with simple honesty. "When I got into court I knew I'd be all right."

George had been vindicated, but the cost to his family had been enormous. On the subject of compensation, the Lords of the Silent Service remained like men without tongues in their heads. In fact, their silence became so marked that it was responsible for acid remarks being made in Parliament.

One speaker voiced the uneasy feelings of many of his fellow members when he declared, "No father in the House would say that ten or twenty thousand pounds would compensate for what has been done." He reminded his listeners: "It is in the discretion of the

First Lord of the Admiralty. So let him get up and do it like a man."

Again, still belatedly the Admiralty made a move with every appearance of being reluctant. They agreed that a sum totalling £7,120 should be paid to cover Martin Archer-Shee's costs and as compensation. Within a few months it was demonstrated that no sum could have saved a life expended in the cause of clearing a boy's name. Martin Archer-Shee's health had been impaired by the frustrations and exertions he had endured in the cause of simple justice. He died some short while after knowing he had not exerted himself in vain.

Within a short time the First World War had broken out. One of the first khaki-clad young officers to fall fighting in the British lines was George Archer-Shee.

He was nineteen.

A MATTER OF HIGH TREASON

In 1911, a year after George Archer-Shee ceased to be a liability to the conscience of British justice, the British Consul-General in Rio de Janeiro received a letter from his departmental chief, announcing that he had been accorded a knighthood for his work in the service of Britain.

Only five years after that, the same man was tried as a traitor to Britain. He was found guilty of high treason in wartime and sentenced to die. The sentence was duly carried out on August 3, 1916, at Pentonville Prison. Outside the prison gates a crowd cheered the news that the hangman had done his job.

The man who received his knighthood in 1911 and died as a traitor in 1916 was a curiously enigmatic Irishman who has been shrewdly described as "the born amateur." His name was Roger Casement.

The tragedy of the man is probably that he got more from Fate than his just deserts. He most likely didn't deserve a knighthood, and possibly he didn't deserve to die.

Unquestionably he was rather a disappointed man by his own thinking, but he had a flair for being noticed, whether for the right or the wrong reason. A product of Ballymena Academy, he had entered the British consular service in 1895, and was sent to bury himself in what was then known as the Dark Continent and the White Man's Grave. But more than once Roger Casement was to prove a difficult man to bury.

Within a decade he had furnished his superiors with a report on Congo atrocities that, when their substance was generally known, became a scandal and an embarrassment to the Belgian monarchy and Government. Possibly he had reservations about the way his intelligence from Africa was received in the corridors of Whitehall. However that may be, he began what amounted almost to a feud with some of the gentlemen using those corridors. In 1910 it seemed a safe policy to send the observant consular official westwards across the Atlantic to South America.

His health had suffered in Africa. It did not improve greatly in Brazil. But then he was using his energies once more to procure the shocking truth about a fresh native scandal. This time his interest was centered on the brutal treatment of the inhabitants of a large stretch of land around the River Putumayo, which was not the responsibility of any South American Government, although no less than four had an interest in its eventual development.

This second uncovering of an atrocity scandal made him popular in certain radical circles in Britain. When he came back to England he was a man receiving homage from admirers. But he was not in a mood to be particularly receptive. His antipathy to Whitehall had grown with the years, paralleled by a deterioration in his health. His thoughts turned towards retirement and what he could do with his leisure. In 1913, for medical reasons, he was granted a lengthy leave of absence, and he went to Dublin and made conversation over food with the man who had called himself Major MacBridie, the leader of the Irish Brigade that had made common cause with the Boers. This move revealed a change in Casement's views over the past dozen years. He was intrigued by the talk of Irish nationalism, and at the end of his leave and return to Rio he soon made arrangements to retire on medical grounds. These grounds were actually rather flimsy. However, the British Foreign Office accepted them.

Sir Roger Casement, already something of a stormy petrel, had become a bird of passage. He left the consular service and journeyed to comfortable surroundings in Ireland, where he had the time to indulge his fancy and feelings in bright talk of rebellion. He continued to New York, where he was greeted by a kindred spirit, a German-born professor, who had been afforded refuge by Britain when he left his native land to avoid being called up for military service. Professor Meyer returned only hatred for the kindnesses he had received and the good livelihood he had been afforded in Liverpool.

In 1914, while Casement was still receiving his British pension, he was preparing to visit Germany, after being assured that war was imminent. When at last he sailed from the United States for Europe he had a scheme for raising an Irish Brigade of his own. He had joined Professor Meyer in his hatred of Britain. Through Von Bernstorff, the Kaiser's ambassador in Washington, arrangements were made for Professor Meyer's brother Richard to take charge of the Irish bird of passage when he arrived in Berlin.

Casement left for Europe on October 15, 1914, a passenger in the Norwegian ship *Oscar II*. He sailed in the company of a certain Adler Christensen, an effeminate person who has been discribed as a degenerate with a painted face. The pair made an odd appearance when they arrived in Norway, after *Oscar II* had been intercepted by a patrolling British warship. Casement was using the false name of James Lundy when he reached Norwegian soil, where he was nearly kidnapped in a plot devised by the British Minister. The journey to Berlin was something of a comedy of errors.

In the wartime German capital the comedy progressed with fewer errors but possibly more farce. Casement could not speak German well enough to converse, and his scheme for an Irish Brigade was not taken seriously until batches of Irish soldiers serving with the British forces were taken prisoner.

In January 1915 he arrived at their camp. Instead of having his call to arms greeted with the enthusiasm he expected, he found he had to be protected from short-tempered prisoners of war who had small time for traitors. Casement's cause was a lost one before it began. A few Irish priests who had come from Italy tried to further the work he had almost begun. They took months to raise a brigade of fifty men, most of whom joined in order to procure better living conditions, food and rates of pay than prisoners of war enjoyed under the terms of the Geneva Convention. In a long-view perspective of nearly half a century they have been described as "the dregs of the British Army."

His mission a failure, Casement remained for a year something of a bad joke to his German hosts. His cabin companion, the

Norwegian Christensen, grew tired of Europe, especially of wartime Germany and found his way back to the United States. Deserted, Casement entertained fresh thoughts of another move for himself. He mentioned this to some officials and was promptly informed he could have a passport that would take him to Sweden or Switzerland. The Germans seemed indelicately ready to see the last of him. Before he came to any decision, he had to spend some time in a Munich sanatorium.

He was there in March 1916 when an Irish-American visited him with news of the intended Easter Rising in Dublin, for which the Germans were sparing a shipload of weapons and ammunition. Only when an enthusiastic Casement reached Berlin did he realize the truth. The arms the Germans were prepared to send to Ireland for use by rebels were outdated rifles for the most part, captured from the retreating Russians on the Eastern Front. It is said he tried to warn the Sinn Feiners about the poor quality of German aid, but that his letters were intercepted.

However, twelve days before the Easter Monday, April 24, that was to be D Day for the rising, he sailed in the German submarine U-20 with two other Irishmen. She was the U-boat that had changed history by sinking the *Lusitania* off the southern coast of Ireland. This time she was headed for Tralee Bay, but had to put into Heligoland when her engines broke down and required immediate repairs. Casement and the two other Irishmen were transferred to the U-19. He set foot on Irish soil on Good Friday, the day H.M.S. *Bluebell* from Queenstown intercepted the German ship with the Russian rifles. The German ship was flying the Norwegian flag. Seeing the arms-running game was over, her captain told his crew to scuttle the bogus Norwegian freighter *Aud.*

Casement watched the U-19 vanish under the grey waters of Tralee Bay, and made for a place of concealment. He was found there, in an ancient stone stockade known as McKenna's Fort, by two members of the Irish constabulary who had been told about a mysterious stranger in the neighborhood. At the time he was picked up, Casement had a black bag with a green flag, field glasses, and some ammunition. On the way to Tralee he tore up a piece of paper containing a complicated code. This was later recovered, as was the overcoat he had concealed in a hedge at McKenna's Fort. In one pocket was found the duplicate of his first class ticket for a sleeping compartment from Berlin to the port of Wilhelmshaven.

Casement's amateur status as a renegade British subject was never made more obvious than in his lack of attention to important details on the U-boat trip to meet his destiny. He had shaved off his trim beard, but this concession to the necessity for disguise was of little avail. In Tralee he was recognized from a newspaper photo. When his identity was known, instructions soon arrived to send him to Dublin for early passage to London.

In London, evidence of his activities in Germany had been received from exchanged Irish prisoners of war who had listened to the man trying to induce them to join an Irish Brigade to fight beside their captors.

Sir Richard Casement was wanted as a traitor. He was a British subject who had sided with the enemies of his country in wartime.

He was also a very careless man and a most unlucky one. He had even been out of luck in his choice of companions aboard the U-19. One of them stayed in hiding after Casement's arrest and bided his time to reach the United States. The other, Daniel Bailey, was rounded up and sent to England to join Casement in custody. To save himself, he readily told his captors all he knew about the plot involving Casement, himself, and the other. It was little enough, but his recanting saved him from standing trial, and he did not have to appear in court as a witness against Casement at the latter's trial.

This opened two months after the U-19 had put Casement ashore in a dinghy, which had been found by a farmer named John McCarthy, and a little more than a month after his being committed for trial at Bow Street.

The trial was, in the legal phrase, at Bar, which means that a minimum of three judges sat on the Bench. The Lord Chief Justice, Lord Reading, who as Rufus Isaacs had dramatically closed the Archer-Shee hearing, presided. He was assisted by Mr. Justice Horridge and Mr. Justice Avory. In charge of presenting the Crown's case was the Attorney General, the brilliant F. E. Smith who later became Lord Birkenhead. He had a number of distinguished assistants, including the later Sir Archibald Bodkin, the

Director of Public Prosecutions. Leading a notable defense panel was Serjeant Sullivan, a prominent representative of the Irish Bar. One of his assistants was an American lawyer named Doyle.

The actual opening was dramatic enough. It was marked by Serjeant Sullivan challenging the jury chosen for the case. As the buoyant challenger pointed out, no one at the English Bar had ever sat through a jury being challenged, while equally no one attending an Irish courtroom hearing could remember when the jury went unchallenged. The American helping him was quick to smile his appreciation of the point. It is common practice in American courts to take days selecting a jury who might be challenged repeatedly by both prosecution counsel and counsel for the defense.

However, once the hearing had started it suffered a setback when one of the jurors became ill and had to be excused. It meant picking a fresh jury and beginning again. When once the witnesses for the Crown started to appear, they were thoroughly cross-examined by Serjeant Sullivan, who seemed to treat them as though they could alter the quality of the high treason with which the prisoner was charged. What seemed curious to some observers was that the defense, aware that the prisoner had admitted committing acts which in English law were treasonable for a British subject, made almost no point of the basic grounds he had for pleading not guilty —which was, being an Irishman, that he was not subject to English law.

That was the arch which either supported the prisoner and freed him or collapsed under him and put his life in jeopardy.

"The real interest to a lawyer," said the Earl of Birkenhead years later, "was the point whether any offense had been committed. Mr. Sullivan took the point before the prisoner pleaded, but the court thought the best course was to hear the evidence first, because then the facts would be fully before the court. Consequently when I closed the case for the prosecution the legal argument began."

The chief argument to engage both sides in the trial of Sir Roger Casement for high treason was about the true meaning of a statute that had become law more than six hundred years before and had been drawn up not in English, but Norman-French.

But before reaching the bone of fiercest legal contention, the Attorney General had been scathing in his reference to the prisoner's activity in trying to start the Irish Brigade among prisoners of war in Germany.

He said: "Whether it entered Casement's head that he was exposing poor men, his inferiors in education and knowledge of the world, to penalties of high treason I do not know. Whether he conceived of the innocent blood which was soon to flow in the unhappy country to which he professed devotion I cannot tell you. But he repeatedly addressed those prisoners of war."

He continued on a fine note of sarcasm: "I do not think it likely that he dwelt upon his connection with a country that had afforded him with a career, which had decorated him with a title, and from which he drew a pension." I suspect that he did not tell them that three years before he had sent his humble duty to the Sovereign, whose soldiers, while their hearts were heavy in captivity, he was attempting to seduce and corrupt."

They were calculated references to the man on trial, for the Attorney General knew that what he said would be reported later in the newspapers of the United States, which even as he made them was facing up to the possibility of waging war against the nation responsible for the sinking of the *Lusitania*. One of his most telling comments for American reading was made when he said:

"The Germans were evidently not concerned to use Casement for the purpose of forming a brigade in order to add one more to the uniforms, already considerable in number, in the German Army. The inference will probably be drawn that it was intended that such men as could be seduced from their allegiance should form the first fruits of a body which should be used for the purpose of raising armed insurrection in Ireland against the forces of the Crown, and of acting as a trained and instructed nucleus round which the disaffected section of the population might rally and grow. Surely in that unhappy country, which has been the victim of so many cruel and cynical conspiracies, never was a conspiracy more cruel and cynical than this."

The language used by the future Earl of Birkenhead might sound dated today, but the condemnation comes through clearly. The language of the time of Edward III was even more dated and still more significant to the prisoner's case.

"If a man do levy war against our lord the King in his realm," says the statute that became a theme for argument between prosecution and defense, "or be adherent to the King's enemies in his realm giving comfort to them aid or comfort in the realm or elsewhere and therefore be attainted . . ."

Lawyers have always been noted for a preference for a minimum of punctuation. They certainly were when those words were first written in Norman-French. Because of the legal shyness for commas, that description of a traitor can be read to mean a number of different conditions, some more legally damning than others. The argument became—could Casement be considered a traitor if his adherence to the King's enemies occurred only when he was outside the realm? The defense said no. The prosecution said it did not matter whether he was inside or outside the realm because both conditions were covered by the statute. The defense pointed out that, if one read commas into the all-important phrase, and if these commas acted as parenthesis, then the prisoner at the bar of the court was not covered by the interpretation of the phrase made by the prosecution.

The wrangle developed until the listening jurors were bemused. The three eminent judges had to make a decision in law. They did this by reference to the precedents of earlier trials and previous rulings. In this they had the more than willing cooperation of an Attorney General who had done his legal homework. The history of some notorious traitors was raked over like newly cleared soil.

The defense put up by Serjeant Sullivan crumpled, and he desperately shifted his legal ground and argued that the prisoner had not sought to aid Germany in the war with Britain. He had sought only to recruit Irishmen to fight for Ireland. Striving to dig in on a new defense line, he appealed to the jury.

"These Irish soldiers," he reminded them, "were never seen marching or countermarching or indulging in sham fights under the command of any German officer. They never appeared in arms to the detriment of any of His Majesty's subjects."

He paused and took a breath before adding, "I ask you to believe that what was done was never of the smallest aid or comfort to the German Government."

The courtroom adversaries were continuing to use the translated Norman-French phrasing. "Aid and comfort" was a phrase that by repetition in that court came to acquire throughout the trial a curiously embellished quality, like something highly polished with hard wear. The jury, being ordinary men conditioned to the everyday exigencies of their immediate world, could be forgiven for appearing more concerned with the parade of evidence that told the story of Casement's activities over that historical Easter until his capture.

One of the four days of the trial was taken up by the total of legal arguments. The Lord Chief Justice, at the close of the testimony and arguments, gave a very careful and balanced summing-up for the benefit of the jury, who were instructed that in the present case, if treason had been proved in fact, then it had been treason within the law's meaning.

Given this guide, the jury did not require long to make up their minds about Roger Casement's treason. They brought in their verdict of guilty against a prisoner who had not chosen to go into the witness box and speak on his own behalf. However, with the verdict delivered, and a fateful die cast, Casement decided he had to put up some sort of show, and he made a speech. It was slanted at Irishmen in Ireland. It was rhetorical in condemning the twentieth-century usage of a fourteenth-century statute that did not apply to Irishmen. The speech went on for a long time with no one interrupting.

Only when Casement had finished was sentence delivered. Sir Roger Casement was to be hanged. The man who had been so rhetorical against English law decided to appeal to another English Court. Two weeks after he had been sentenced to death six judges of the Court of Criminal Appeal, led by Mr. Justice Darling, heard the appeal brought by Sir Roger Casement and dismissed it. Leave to appeal to the House of Lords was refused by the Attorney General, who had this to say on the subject years later:

After the most careful and anxious reconsideration I came to the decided opinion that I ought not to shrink from the responsibility of refusing the application, and accordingly no further appeal took place.

As a rider to this acknowledgment he added:

It was no part of my duty to consider whether the King should show any leniency to the prisoner. There can be no question that the decision not to interfere with the execution of the sentence was right. Casement, blinded by hatred of this country, as malignant in quality as it was sudden in origin, had played a desperate hazard in our hour of need. He had lost, and his life was forfeit.

Roger Casement was hanged on August 3, 1916, and on the next day, the second anniversary of the outbreak of war between Germany and Great Britain, there was a formal announcement that before Casement's execution the King had withdrawn the honors previously granted a condemned traitor.

Today, more than half a century after the trial and execution of a man who had been a baffling contemporary to many, there is a still-argued outcome of those disturbed days of fear and tension. The argument concerns whether or not certain entries in diaries left in Casement's former lodging in Ebury Street, London, were forged or not. They were found by detectives who searched the rooms some time after their writer had been arrested. They were taken to Sir Basil Thomson, who was at that time the Assistant Commissioner at New Scotland Yard. He was a man who was to grow used to dealing with spies and traitors. On one notable occasion he even gave the notorious Mata Hari some well-intended advice to stop her dangerous game of playing off the French against the Germans. He said of certain passages in the Casement diaries that "they could not be printed in any language."

Today, the argument persists about those passages. Some partisans maintain that unsavory passages dealing with Casement's personal life, details of his relationships with other men while in the consular service, were inserted in order to create a favorable impression in the United States for the outcome of the trial. However, as a similar diary was discovered sometime afterward in Ireland, where no forger could have obtained access to it, the argument is not always supported by the array of evidence that can be shown.

This is not necessarily a deterrent to those who are anxious to resurrect the strange man who died at Pentonville in early August 1916. As late as 1969 the work of presenting Roger Casement as a martyr continued apace, when a play entitled *The Royal Rape of Ruari MacAmund* was produced in New York. Ruari MacAmund was the Gaelic version of Casement's name.

But if the present-day defenders are heated in their assertions, those who feel that the man received his just deserts are no less cool in their employment of logic and facts. Handwriting tests have decided the argued and debated passages were not forgeries. Of the diaries still in existence, it is possible for students to obtain permission to study them as basic human documents.

However, not all remain to be examined.

One was destroyed by a close friend of Casement's, Francis Biggar, who after the trial went through a number of personal papers belonging to the condemned man. They had been left in Biggar's safe-keeping together with an additional volume of the diaries that cover the years 1903, 1910, and 1911. Besides the diaries proper, there is a black ledger of rather small size, crammed with Casement's writing, and a notebook. The volume Biggar had in his keeping was found by him to be so disturbing when he started to read it that he burned it together with the other Casement papers in his possession.

He felt it was the least he could do to protect the good name of an unhappy man he had once called his friend.

The diaries today are a subject often employed to confuse an issue that the trial proved to be simple and clear-cut when reduced to legal essentials. Roger Casement was a traitor and was convicted as such and sentenced to death. Any curious perversions in which he indulged in no way operated for or against his guilt or innocence. However, the defenders of Casement today tend to ignore one rather significant detail. When the diaries were discovered and their unsavory contents became known, they were shown to the men responsible for Casement's defense. If Casement's counsel believed such entries pointed to the writer being of unsound mind, then there was the possibility of the prisoner being found insane.

Casement was told. He denied that he had written the entries, and his counsel accepted his word. In those circumstances there was no question of going ahead with the plea of insanity.

So the trial continued with the now notorious diaries a subject kept secret from the jury and the general public alike. But after Casement's death the secret became widely discussed until it was common knowledge. Not until 1966 were the diaries allowed to be viewed by responsible students. By that time Roger Casement had become a subject for legend and top-heavy martyrdom, rather like his curious other self, Ruari MacAmund.

THE GREEN BICYCLE MYSTERY

The trial of Ronald Light for murder was held at Leicester Assizes in 1920. For fifty years it has remained an object lesson for students of trials and murder cases. The trial closed with Ronald Light being freed and Sir Edward Marshall Hall, a truly formidable courtroom figure, scoring one of his notable triumphs.

Today the murder of Bella Wright remains unsolved. Numerous individuals have put forward theories to provide a solution to the mystery of her death, and on one occasion I had an anonymous writer offer to interest me in the inside story of a person, once closely connected with the case, who was, the writer claimed, still receiving "a pension" for continued silence.

The case opened at half-past nine on a summer evening. The date was July 5, 1919. At that hour a farmer named Cowell was driving some cows along the old Roman road known as the Via Devana, about five miles to the southeast of Leicester. In the light of the westering sun he saw a young girl lying in the road ahead. Beside her was a bicycle. The girl was dead.

The farmer, shocked by his discovery, hurried to inform the local constable, a level-headed man named Hall who promptly summoned a doctor. By the time the first examination of the body was completed, the light had faded from the sky. The girl's death was thought to have been accidental. Constable Hall returned to the Roman road early the following morning. He examined the surface where the body had been found, located the bicycle tracks, and came upon something startling—a revolver bullet. He reported his find and the body was again examined. This time, under a scab of dried blood below the dead girl's left eye, the doctor found a bullet hole.

The girl had been shot dead. The police had to find her murderer.

Thanks to Constable Hall's conscience in the matter of duty, the police had a reasonably early start in looking for the killer, but they quickly discovered there was no recognizable trail to follow.

The dead girl was soon identified as a factory worker who had been engaged on a night shift in Leicester. Her name was Bella Wright. She was twenty-one, had been endowed with youthful good looks and had the reputation of a modest young woman of a friendly disposition. She had lived with her parents in the village of Stoughton, through which runs the Via Devana, and on the evening of her death she had left home about half-past six to cycle to her uncle's house in the hamlet of Gaulby, which is about nine miles east of Leicester. She had arrived at her uncle's about half-past seven. When she left, her uncle, a road-mender named Measures, stepped outside his front door to see her cycle down the road. He was surprised to see her accompanied by a young man on another bicycle. It was a vivid green.

There was a step behind him, and he turned to see his son-in-law, James Evans, a miner, who was very handy at fixing bicycles.

"That's the chap she told us about, isn't it?" said the older man.

The younger nodded, but he was straining to catch the words being spoken to Bella. He thought he heard the young man on the green bicycle say, "Bella, you have been a long time," accenting the third word.

When detectives interviewed the uncle and his son-in-law they were told that Bella, when she arrived, had told them a young man had ridden up to her and tried to start a conversation.

She had said, "Perhaps if I wait a while he will be gone."

But the young man with the green bicycle had been waiting outside the cottage when she left. He rode off in her company. Thirty-five minutes later the farmer found her body lying bathed in blood and dying sunlight, with her bicycle lying at an angle beside her.

The police, provided with this information, tried to locate the young man who had joined Annie Bella Wright on her ride to Gaulby and who had left when she did. He seemed the likeliest suspect and the possible owner of the revolver that had fired the bullet that killed her. Whatever his motive, he had not assaulted the girl. When found, her clothes were not disarranged and she was still wearing her hat. These details had helped to suggest that her death was due to a cycling accident when Constable Hall and the doctor first came upon the body.

But now the police had a mystery. They had to find a killer and then establish his motive for shooting the young woman. Accident or murder? The former, in the view of the police, seemed unlikely. But only when they found the man who had pedalled off on a distinctive green bicycle down the flat lanes east of Leicester would they have the answer they sought.

The police began calling at village front doors. They came upon two small girls who told them they had been stopped by a young man on a green bicycle on the afternoon of July 5. All effort was directed to locating the green bicycle that had been well described by James Evans. Throughout the next few days owners of green bicycles in and around Leicester found themselves explaining their movements on the afternoon and evening of July 5. The inquiry did not find the particular green bicycle ridden by Bella's companion on the fatal evening.

The Leicestershire police called in Scotland Yard to assist in the manhunt, and almost immediately a reward of twenty pounds was offered for information that would lead to the identification of the green bicycle's rider.

Christmas came and went, with the police still in possession of only one promising clue, the fact of the green bicycle, which seemed to have vanished. Then, on February 23, 1920, there was a further startling development in a case which had first made headlines in the national press, then been pushed aside for more topical news. On that day a boatman working a canal saw his tow rope suddenly go slack, drop under the water, then become taut again, like a fishing line when the bait has been taken. Hanging on the taut tow rope, to the boatman's astonished gaze, was part of a bicycle.

He had just time to glimpse it and to gain the impression that it was green before the rope released what it had hooked.

The boatman continued with his load of coal, which was to be delivered at the same factory where Bella Wright had worked on the night shift. The next day he returned to the place where his tow rope had been fouled and began dragging for that curious find. He was a determined man who had read about the missing green bicycle and the reward of twenty pounds that had been offered by the police. He kept dragging the water until again he hooked what he had found on the previous day.

It was indeed part of a green bicycle.

Moreover, it fitted James Evans's description of a bicycle made to a special order and with readily distinguishable features. What seemed curious was that most of the more readily discernible identification marks had been scraped away, leaving patches of bare metal. But whoever had taken those precautions had missed the extra identification number added to the pillar of the handlebar bracket. This could be made out quite clearly.

The number was 103648.

Now the police really did some intensive routine detective work, and they discovered that a bicycle with this number had been sold in Birmingham to a Mr. Light ten years before, in 1910.

By this time a more systematic dragging of the canal had been undertaken and further pieces of the green bicycle were recovered as well as a revolver holster containing cartridges. Inquiries moved closer to the Via Devana, and detectives found a bicycle repair shop in Leicester where a green bicycle with the number of the machine recovered in pieces from the canal was remembered. Three days before the finding of Bella's body, the bicycle had been brought to the shop for a repairing job.

The man who had brought the green bicycle was a Mr. Light.

It seemed that the police inquiry had come full circle and in the center of that circle was a man named Light who had some explaining to do.

Finding him was no difficult task. It was learned that Ronald Light was a schoolmaster working at a school in Cheltenham. Formerly he had lived in Leicester with his mother. The assistant master answering to the full name of Ronald Vivian Light showed considerable surprise when one morning he was visited by a detective inspector named Taylor who had a number of very pertinent questions to ask him. The first was, had he purchased a B.S.A. bicycle in Birmingham on May 13, 1910?

Ronald Light seemed flustered at Inspector Taylor's direct approach. He told the detective he had never been the owner of a green bicycle, and went on to state that he had not been in the region of Gaulby on July 5 last year and had never known a young woman named Bella Wright. Pressed about his answers, he admitted later that he had in fact once owned a green bicycle, but he had sold it a long time ago.

Ronald Light proved less responsive and forthcoming than Inspector Taylor could have wished. Indeed, he created a very bad impression by his vacillating answers which were not supported by information already in the possession of the police.

Not surprisingly, Ronald Light was arrested. He duly appeared to have the case against him heard by a magistrate at Leicester Castle. When the hearing was over, Ronald Light had been committed for trial on a charge of murder.

To most readers of the newspapers at that time, the case looked open-and-shut. For the man who had been arrested had been identified by both Measures and James Evans as the young man who had waited on his green bicycle for Bella to leave the cottage and return home.

The one element of remaining mystery, it seemed from a statement made by Light's counsel at the magistrate's hearing, was whether or not the prisoner could produce an alibi. The trial at which the public's curiosity would be appeased opened on June 10, eleven months after Bella Wright had been shot dead.

Leading the defense was Marshall Hall. Opposing him for the Crown was the Attorney General, Sir Gordon Hewart. Also in the ranks of prosecutors was Norman Birkett, who was about to make his first entry on an important legal stage.

When he rose to open the case the Attorney General went straight into attack. He covered all the significant points that made out the case against the prisoner. Indeed, the case he made out seemed to most of his listeners to be conclusive. Watched closely by the very attentive judge, Mr. Justice Horridge, Sir Gordon posed the question all England had been asking for months passed.

"Who was the man on the green bicycle?"

He went on to claim that the man in the dock was that man. For once it looked as though the imperturbable Marshall Hall might not be able to save his client in the face of such overwhelming testimony as the prosecution prepared to offer for the consideration of the jury.

But to his colleagues of the Bar who knew him well, the famous advocate did not look worried by the magnitude of the defense task confronting him. He did not come forward with any strong challenges for the prosecution witnesses when they took their places in the box. He asked the occasional question, as though to elucidate a detail in his own mind. Possibly, after the rumors that Light's defense would come forward with an alibi, Marshall Hall, with the court issue now joined, realized that no alibi was possible. The identification of Light by the dead girl's uncle and his son-in-law was far too positive.

On the other hand, Marshall Hall quickly disposed of the evidence of the two small girls who claimed to have been accosted earlier on July 5 by a man on a green bicycle. He demonstrated that their evidence was little more than fancy. Mr. Justice Horridge must have been in full agreement, for later, when he had to sum up for the jury, he advised them to pay small attention to the girls' story. Marshall Hall was a past master at sowing seeds of doubt in the minds of puzzled jurors. On this occasion he could do little with the identification of his client by Measures and James Evans, but he did force a time issue when he claimed that they were wrong in the matter of the time when Bella Wright left the cottage to cycle home.

He supported this with another oblique attack on the evidence of the words James Evans had overheard. He suggested that the man they had identified had not said the girl's name, "Bella," but rather the greeting, "Hello." When he put the suggestion to the uncle and his son-in-law neither would agree with him, but people sitting in the courtroom could see that the suggestion had carried some weight with the jury.

It would have been an easy mistake to make, and, furthermore, it would have been honestly made. None knew better than the advocate who had put the suggestion.

However, a challenge to the advocate arose when a Leicester gunsmith, Henry Clarke, was called to give expert testimony for the

Crown. Marshall Hall took full advantage of the opportunity offered him. He understood how an attacking line with expert testimony always impresses a jury.

First he elicited from the gunsmith that the bullet that had killed Bella Wright was of a pattern used very largely since the end of the Boer War. This led up to the gunsmith agreeing that thousands of millions of such bullets had been made in the past two decades. One out of such a number seemed a very small proportion, indeed infinitesimal. Eliciting this information, which was not particularly relevant, was rather like telling the jury so many bullets of this calibre had been made that it was not surprising one had turned up on the Via Devana. This was a reflection calculated to further the case for the prisoner in minds that might be less than needle sharp.

The expert witness was shown the bullet that had taken Bella's life. He told the court it had rifling marks and had been fired from a Webley and Scott revolver. The range of this firearm would be about a thousand yards, and its velocity would allow it to pierce an inch of solid timber at a distance of some fifty to sixty yards.

By this time the jury were sitting forward. Marshall Hall shot a question at the witness.

"Have you ever seen a human being," he asked Henry Clarke, "who has been shot at a distance of within five yards with a Service revolver?"

The man in the witness box shook his head and said he had not.

Then the defense counsel came back at him with, "I suggest that the effect of such a bullet on the skull of a human being is almost to blow the side of the head off?"

The witness was very careful with his answer. "It depends entirely on the velocity, sir," he told Marshall Hall.

This reply didn't satisfy the probing defense counsel, who brought the witness to agree that the part of the head struck by the bullet was an important factor.

Henry Clarke also admitted that this particular bullet could be fired from a rifle as well as a Service revolver of the Webley and Scott type. Here was a doubt created by the wily defense counsel —had the fatal bullet been fired from a revolver or farther away from a rifle? It was a point that remained to be considered by the jury.

In the witness's view the bullet had struck the victim under the eye and passed on through the skull to fall on the road.

Marshall Hall was ready to throw another doubt at the jury when he said, "Would it not go on for several hundred yards?"

"Not," said the witness, "if it went at an acute angle."

Somehow that did not seem the kind of answer to destroy the doubt.

Marshal Hall had found his line of defense and was making the most of it. He was unable to show that the prisoner had not been with the victim, so he concentrated on throwing doubt on the prosecution's certainty that Ronald Light had fired the fatal shot.

The defense counsel pointed out to the jury that a bullet of the precise calibre of the one recovered from the Via Devana could be expected to make a larger hole at the point of entry than the one just able to be filled with an ordinary lead pencil that had been drilled beneath Bella Wright's eye. This was more doubt to engage their minds.

What also had to be done was to undo the damage already made by the prisoner's first statements to the police. Marshall Hall knew very well that only one person could explain the prisoner's earlier lies to the jury's satisfaction, if that were at all possible—the prisoner himself.

So to the surprise of many, he put Ronald Light in the witness box. But the defense counsel was depending on the impression Light would create when asked about his earlier life in the wartime Army. Standing to attention, Light gave his replies in a firm voice without speaking loudly, and did not appear embarrassed by the questions he was asked to answer.

Marshall Hall referred to the revolver Light admitted once possessing.

"Where did you get it from?" he asked.

"I bought it from my commanding officer, Major Benton," said the prisoner.

"What sort was it?" his counsel wanted to know.

"An ordinary Webley-Scott Service revolver."

"Did you take it to France with you?"

"Yes, in 1917."

"What was your capacity then?"

"I was gunner in the Honorable Artillery Company."

"Were you allowed to have a revolver as a private?" Marshall Hall next wanted to know.

"Yes," the prisoner told him, "but you could not wear it, of course."

"What happened to you?" the prisoner's counsel continued.

Light said, "In 1918 I passed through a casualty clearing station at the base."

"How was that?"

"I was sent there for shell shock and deafness. I have been deaf ever since."

The prisoner was by this reply shown in a favorable light as a victim of the recent war. Marshall Hall underlined the effect by next asking, "And then?" and being told, "I remained at the base for two or three days and was sent across to England as a stretcher case."

At this point the defense counsel was ready to introduce the tricky subject of Ronald Light's revolver.

"What was sent with you?" he asked, the examination by this time going like clockwork.

"I came across in my pajamas and my sole possession was a dolly bag, as they call it."

"And the revolver?"

"It was taken away from me with all my other kit and left behind."

"Have you ever seen it since?"

"Never."

The atmosphere in the court was quite tense by this time. The most relaxed person present was the counsel for the defense. He elicited the information for the jury's benefit that the revolver's holster had followed its owner with the latter's kit, but not the weapon itself. Light had spent three months in hospital in England before being demobilized in January 1919, when he went to live with his mother in Leicester.

The jury could only view what it had heard with favor. Striking while a stroke could be effective, Marshall Hall switched his questions to the day, six months later, when Light went bicycling through a number of Leicester villages.

"Did you see a young lady riding a bicycle?" he asked.

There was no hesitation on the prisoner's part. "Yes," he said, and was asked which way she was travelling.

"She was standing by her bicycle at the roadside," was the reply, and Light went on to explain that he did not know her and had never seen her before, whereupon his counsel asked him to tell the jury what took place at the meeting.

"As I got up to the young lady she was stooping over her bicycle," the prisoner said. "She looked up at my approach and asked if I could lend her a wrench. I had no wrenches with me, so I just looked at her machine. As far as I could see there was a certain amount of play with the free-wheel. As I had no wrench I could do nothing about it."

He related how they rode off together, going down one steep hill and up another, at one stage walking side by side. They had come to the village of Gaulby, where the girl told him she was going to visit some friends and would be about ten minutes or a quarter-of-an-hour.

Light said in reply to a question from Marshall Hall: "As she said she would not be long, I took that as a sort of suggestion that I should wait and we should ride on together."

He claimed he had waited a quarter-of-an-hour in a lane between the house where the girl had gone and the nearby church. When he had started to push his bicycle back to the road he found he had a flat tire. He spent about an hour mending it. Then he mounted and rode towards the house and saw the girl leaving it. He rode up and said, "Hello, you've been a long time. I thought you'd gone the other way."

"Did you call her Bella?" Marshall Hall asked.

"No."

"When did you first see her name?" Light was asked.

"When I first read the accounts in the papers," he told the court.

He explained how, on the ride back from Gaulby, his tire went down again and he had to pump it up. The girl rode on slowly, and he overtook her.

"Was there some conversation about tires?" the defense counsel inquired, making his verbal moves with the skill of a chess champion.

"Yes," Light said obediently. "She then told me the first thing I knew about her. It was this. She never let her tires get into such a state as she was employed at a tire factory and could get them at cost price."

They had parted company, he claimed, when she turned away at a road junction, saying, "I must say goodbye to you here. I am going that way."

She had disappeared down the road to the left.

When Marshall Hall turned away from the witness box he seemed pleased. The prosecution was ready to try to undo the favorable impression created under the defense counsel's guidance. It failed. When Light was asked why he had not come forward voluntarily to help the police he said, with the same air of telling a straightforward truth, "Because at first I was absolutely dazed by the whole thing. I did not think clearly about it. I could not make up my mind what to do. Everyone, apparently, jumped to the conclusion that the man with the green bicycle had murdered the girl."

He added that he had been anxious not to worry his mother, and when the judge interposed to ask if he didn't think he could have helped the police he said clearly, "I see that now, my lord," and with his previous candor admitted filing the numbers from his cycle and discarding it in the canal.

That gave the prosecution a chance to get rugged in its tactics and inquire if it wouldn't have been better at the preliminary hearing for him to have been frank then. But this time the judge interposed on the prisoner's behalf to point out that he had been within his rights to reserve his defense.

Mr. Justice Horridge added drily, "If a prisoner sits tight until he's really tried before judge and jury, I think he's often a very wise man."

A few of the faces in the jury box relaxed dutifully.

Marshall Hall, however, was not finished with the jury. When it came time to address them in his closing speech he pointed out that, had the prisoner shot Bella Wright, all he had to claim in his own defense was that the gun had gone off accidentally.

Running his gaze down the length of the jury box, the defense counsel added, "There is not a man, woman, or child who would not have accepted that story. There was the perfect defense if he had needed to invent a defense."

After the doubts had been sown, the reasonableness of the

prisoner's actions was skilfully demonstrated. For were they not the actions of an innocent man?

Marshall Hall was well in his stride when a photographer, aware that the jury was being impressed, tried to record the scene. The judge interrupted to censure such an intrusion. After that interruption Marshall Hall closed his speech. He seemed put out by the incident.

When the jury retired and took their first count of votes, three were found to be in favor of a conviction. But after further discussion that continued for three hours, they were all of one mind. They filed back into the jury box and the foreman rose to give their unanimous verdict.

"Not guilty."

Ronald Light was free to leave the court where for a space of days his life had been in jeopardy. Marshall Hall had saved the neck of a client whom most newspaper readers in Britain considered a doomed man when the trial in Leicester Castle opened.

No additional arrest for Bella Wright's murder was made by the police, and the crime still remains officially unsolved, though a number of wide-ranging theories have been advanced from time to time to account for the presence in the Leicestershire twilight of an unknown marksman who fired a shot that killed a young woman on the Via Devana at a spot where Roman legionaries had trod.

BUCCANEER IN MORNING COAT

While many outstanding swindlers succeed in cocooning themselves in a shimmering element of deceptive mystery, sometimes even of financial glamour, few succeed in creating a veritable legend around their slippery personalities and in having it accepted at a very spurious face value.

One of those incredible few was the son of a tailor's cutter and the sister of a social reformer who was also a pioneer of the early Co-operative Movement. The boy was given an heroic-sounding first name, Horatio. It was a good name for a man bent on creating a legend.

Horatio Bottomley had a shrewd brain and was endowed with particularly nimble wits. While still young he made up his mind that there was more satisfaction to be gained from having someone else cut his clothes rather than for him to acquire the skill to cut the clothes of a stranger. So he did not follow William King Bottomley into an ill-lit backroom in East London and learn to wield a pair of tailor's shears. Nor did he give his youthful mind to social reform except to consider how existing society could be induced to make life easy for a young man eager and ambitious to be wealthy and influential and at the same time popular.

He made the first important break with his immediate family background when he obtained employment in the law offices of a firm of City solicitors. There he came face to face with the moral challenge of successful roguery when he discovered a colleague was a swindler. He realized how easy it was to manipulate people at the same time to lighten their pockets. Instead of condemning the rogue he had secretly unmasked, he stood back mentally and took a long view. He found he could admire the man's ability to enrich himself at other people's expense without his fraud being detected.

The swindler who won young Bottomley's admiration and envy was the chief clerk of the firm employing the youthful newcomer. This unprincipled character had been for years sending out county tax bills that were highly inflated and pocketing the receipts. The books were kept balanced, and no one had the least suspicion that a fair sum of money was annually being paid into the chief clerk's pocket rather than into the town council's coffers.

Young Bottomley set himself to understand how the fraud he had detected could continue undiscovered for year after year. The answer, when he arrived at it, seemed simple. People too willingly accepted pretty pieces of paper at face value. Pieces of paper measuring only a few inches square could be exchanged for cash—so long as the people handing over the cash believed the pieces of paper were worth the price.

Bottomley was twenty-one when he joined the firm of Walpoles, legal stenographers under contract to the Law Courts; to his knowledge of how money was readily paid for share certificates, he added experience of how the men of law conducted their business, of how trials were won and lost, and why some eminent judges were to be more feared than others.

Bottomley, through his employment and the practical everyday experience he gained from it, became in time a fairly good lay lawyer. He acquired a persuasive legal jargon as he had previously learned the terminology of City banking houses. By the time he was twnety-nine he was ready to try his specially acquired skill. He and some friends set up the Hansard Publishing Union. The year was 1889.

The pretty pieces of paper appeared when this company became associated with the Anglo-Austrian Publishing Union, which purchased for the sum of £88,000 some properties situated in Vienna. Whether the bricks and mortar in the city of Strauss were genuinely acquired is extremely unlikely. The pretty pieces of paper began changing hands, as did considerable sums of cash. That £ 88,000 vanished like steam in warm sunshine. Horatio Bottomley and his friends suddenly had cash to squander and fresh ideas to exploit.

For four years he used commercial frauds as stepping-stones to a sizable bank balance. Then he got his feet wet by stepping on an insecure stone.

Through an agent he had bought some properties in England, including a firm of Devon printers, for just under a quarter of a million pounds. The Hansard Union bought them for well over that sum. But the properties so obtained and resold were rundown and practically worthless. By the time the directors of the Hansard Union discovered they had been fed lies by a clever sales promoter, their shareholders had lost a great deal of money.

The scandal could not be hushed up, and Bottomley was brought to court. He demonstrated his confidence in himself by conducting his own defense before Mr. Justice Hawkins. Largely due to the reluctance of certain key witnesses to make themselves appear foolish in court, something the shrewd Bottomley was depending on, he won his case.

Instead of going to prison he went into Mr. Justice Hawkins's private chambers to hear some advice offered gratis by a man who was not only a legal luminary of his day, but one with a wide knowledge of rogues of all kinds.

The learned judge told the successful defendant in a very dubious case: "You have exceptional gifts. If you continue to exploit them in the City, such is your nature, you will one day find yourself in one of Her Majesty's prisons. But if you will study law and be admitted to the Bar, you may become one of the great advocates of your day. Think it over."

Bottomley had already done so. He turned his back on the hard grind of becoming a barrister. He was a young man in a hurry to get rich.

By not taking the advice of Mr. Justice Hawkins he was, almost a generation later, to prove the judge a true prophet.

In those thirty years the name of Horatio Bottomley was to become a household word throughout Britain. He divided his attention between the City and Fleet Street. In the City he organized companies and dabbled with the pretty pieces of paper which his eloquence could sell for substantial cash payments. In the street of ink he dabbled in pretty phrases on plain sheets of paper, and Horatio Bottomley achieved the popularity he had sought through the medium of sensational journalism. First with his newspaper the *Sun*, then with his attacking popular weekly, *John Bull*, he couched his message for the man who wanted to believe there was someone looking after his interests. Bottomley directed his journalism not only to the man in the street, but to the man in the mine and the pub and the factory and the workshop. He dealt in scandals. He purported to expose rogues. He offered himself as the fearless protector of the downtrodden. The circulation of *John Bull* soared until it became a journal with political influence.

That was when Horatio Bottomley decided to enter Parliament.

In 1906 he was elected the Liberal Member of Parliament for a London constituency, South Hackney. As financier, journalist and MP he kept himself before the public gaze. He made enemies but also sold himself to millions of ordinary men and women who believed in his flamboyant speeches, his John Bullish jingoism, and especially in his promises of what he could do for those who trusted him.

He created companies into which the public poured money in exchange for more of the pretty pieces of paper. He also created a public image of Horatio William Bottomley, the average man's friend and champion. He became a buccaneer in a morning coat. His appearance in a hall to deliver a speech was greeted with noisy bursts of enthusiasm. He paraded himself as the soul of honest endeavor in the cause of his country and his fellow man. It was all so high-sounding and high-flown that only a hypocrite could have continued in the role with success.

Horatio Bottomley enjoyed a very long run for other people's money.

His great opportunity came with the declaration of war in August 1914. Before the first shots had been fired he was denouncing the enemy and calling upon the British nation to rally to the cause of justice and humanity.

He became one of the greatest recruiting agents of all time. He could do this because he had sold himself to the general public. They accepted him because they believed in him, in what he told them, in what he proclaimed he stood for. Moreover, the man who had founded both *John Bull* and the *Financial Times* was obviously unique.

His uniqueness extended to his private life. He had his country home, the Dicker, in Sussex, where his wife had lived and from which he frequently sortied as the local squire who was a popular local figure seldom shy of dipping his hand into his pocket. He also had a flat not far from Pall Mall, in the heart of London. Here he welcomed and entertained influential figures of the day who could further his schemes for self-advancement. From this luxuriously appointed town home he made a different kind of sortie. It was usually one that took him to the home of a lady of good looks and great discretion, for the man who was making money with great facility, whose health was drunk in both clubs and pubs, was a very social animal and enjoyed company, particularly female.

He bought racehorses and appeared at race meetings in his morning coat, ready to doff his high hat to ladies who were graceful and gracious. He was a figure the ordinary man envied. He was what the ordinary man would like to become, given the chance.

He knew that and traded on the knowledge. For a time the fact almost transmuted him into a hero, one with a palate for both kippers and champagne.

His horse, Northern Farmer, won the Steward's Cup at Goodwood and Bottomley was said to have pocketed £50,000 because his jockey's mount was at the winning post a neck in front of the horse that came second. Another of his racehorses, Wargrave, was believed to have enriched him by a much larger sum when it won the Cesarewitch. No hero ever diminished his stature in the eyes of the British working man by being a good sportsman and a successful gambler. Horatio Bottomley was indeed seen as both.

He put up the money for a number of West End theatrical productions. Most of them were musical shows that appealed to a wide popular audience.

This was the man who became a legend, about whom scores of stories were told. In most of those stories he was joined by other well-known figures. For instance, it was said that on one occasion Bottomley consulted Marshall Hall about a case concerning a lottery run by his paper the *Sun*. After hearing Bottomley's account of the facts, the famous advocate said, "There's only one counsel who will do you justice in this case."

"Tell me who he is," Bottomley asked.

"Yourself," said Marshall Hall.

The story has considerable point when it is recalled that on a number of occasions when Bottomley had to defend a charge in court he was aided by Marshall Hall, who would rise after Bottomley had spoken brilliantly on his own behalf and amuse the court by such an opening phrase as, "Following my unlearned leader . . ."

The pair made a very formidable courtroom team.

With the end of the First World War, Bottomley sought to consolidate his success as a national figure. He had survived court actions and sniping in the press. He was seen by the man in the street as someone who had worked hard to make victory possible.

Then a pamphlet was published with a curious title. It was by Reuben Bigland and was a very different kind of *exposé* from anything printed in *John Bull*. The title was *What Bottomley Did for Britain During the War*. One turned over the title page to find the inside pages empty.

The inference was unavoidable.

The first pamphlet issued by this Birmingham printer made little impact, but it raised a few smiles. The Birmingham printer was a crusader and he issued further pamphlets, all attacking the man who had become a legend. Reuben Bigland wanted to be taken to court by the man he was crusading against. But Bottomley did not sue for criminal slander. The man who had become known to many men in different walks of life by his initials H. B. ignored both slanders and innuendoes. When Bigland printed that Bottomley had been paid the handsome sum of £24,000 for making his electrifying recruiting speeches during the war, no denial was offered.

Bigland decided to involve himself more directly. He wrote a fresh pamphlet in which he stated that during the years 1918-21 Bottomley had procured the vast sum of £1,300,000 of public money. He went on to claim that in one of Bottomley's famous bond draws he himself, Reuben Bigland, had been declared the 'winner' of a £1,000 bond drawn in the contest.

Bottomley continued to sit tight and not be angered into speedy action he could later regret. But by this time it took several bottles of champagne to get him thinking in his own best interests. The late Sir Travers Humphreys, who prosecuted Bottomley in 1922, has put the following on record: "I have been lauded as having done something wonderful in getting Bottomley convicted in 1922. In truth it was not I who floored Bottomley, it was drink. The man I met in 1922 was a drinksodden creature whose brain would only be got to work by repeated doses of champagne."

The hero not only had feet of clay, he had lungs full of alcohol fumes. It was only a question of time before he collapsed. This was a secret he strove to keep from his admirers among the general public, the kind of people who back in 1915 had responded to Bottomley's John Bull War Loan Club, which had been launched from the neutral city of Lucerne, in Switzerland. When the so-called club ran into trouble from the Postmaster General, it was changed into a scheme for selling premium bonds. These bonds were provided by public subscription to purchase the new War Savings Certificates issued by the British Government. The interest on such certificates was used as cash prizes for those who drew lucky numbers. The amount of money flowing into the scheme was never known except to Bottomley and a few of his closest aides. Another similar scheme was the War Stock Consolation Draw, run on almost identical lines. The war had served to fill Bottomley's pockets at a time when they were showing the results of his former extravagance.

With the end of hostilities and the issue of a Government-backed Victory Loan, a further opportunity to collect subscribers into one of his so-called clubs was offered and promptly taken by the conniving buccaneer in morning coat. The bonds were issued in denominations of five pounds, for which a purchase price of fifteen shillings less was asked, and were to be redeemed by annual installments. Bottomley immediately saw the potential wealth of the persons who could not find the capital for investing in paid-up bonds of the Victory Loan. Accordingly he evolved a Victory Bond Club, which his journal *John Bull* announced to the public. Subscribers joining the club were offered the opportunity to secure one-fifth shares in fully priced bonds for fifteen shillings and six-pence, which would earn a full pound on redemption. Again the familiar prizes were offered subscribers from the accrued interest, and the prizes would be drawn periodically. The Victory Bond Club caught both the imagination and the avarice of the public. There was a scramble to invest. By August 1919, nine months after the close of hostilities, nearly half a million pounds had been poured into the scheme.

Bottomley was a shrewd publicist. He believed in gimmicks before the word was coined. The sort of publicity stunt he indulged in was demonstrated when he was offered the German U-boat *Deutschland* by a crony named Pemberton Billing, who had bought the vessel for scrap metal for five thousand pounds. Bottomley bought the war relic for his paper *John Bull,* and paid a price of twelve thousand pounds. The cheque in payment was drawn on the booming Victory Bond Club, and thereafter the U-boat was exhibited in various parts of the country in an effort to whip up enthusiasm for the club. He was even ready with a promise to give subscribers to the club what were called victory trophies, to be made from the *Deutschland's* hull when she was broken up.

In all, Bottomley secured nearly three-quarters of a million subscribers to this new Victory Bond Club. Reuben Bigland, still sniping at Bottomley without hitting a vulnerable target, began using more deadly verbal ammunition.

In a new pamphlet addressed to the Victory Bond Club members he said scathingly: "The British Government has allowed one of the greatest crooks ever born to issue as one-pound shares nearly a million of these pieces of common blue paper."

The pretty pieces of paper had given way to a more utilitarian appearance. But as Bigland pointed out, the issue of them had been accomplished without the aid of trustees or auditors. Reluctantly Bottomley admitted he was being pushed into a position where he had to act. The goaded editor of *John Bull* knew instinctively that he would regret taking legal action against Bigland, but he was snared by circumstances no longer controlled by himself.

Marshall Hall was retained to appear for Bottomley when the action against Bigland came to court. However, on the morning of the trial, Bigland's defending counsel, Mr. Comyns-Carr, called on Marshall Hall with a briefcase full of documents. Marshall Hall glanced through them and at once hurried to see Bottomley.

"We're offering no evidence," he informed his client. "It's the only course to take, and there's nothing you can do about it."

Marshall Hall added that unless Bottomley took his advice he would withdraw from the case, and if Bottomley did take his advice the editor of *John Bull* would not go into the witness box and risk being cross-examined. Marshall Hall had seen sufficient in the documents he had been shown to realize that this time Bottomley would be a loser. Bottomley himself knew it.

"They'll prosecute me," he said.

Marshall Hall didn't contradict him. Instead he echoed his client's gloomiest fears.

"That's inevitable," he told Bottomley.

However, he did his barrister's best for his client on the January day in 1922 when he surprised the court by asking for an adjournment because the books of the Victory Bond Club were in the hands of the receivers. Bigland, the defendant in this action for criminal libel, had pleaded not guilty. Because of this Marshall Hall, the wily legal skirmisher, refused to agree to the defendant reading a plea which would have successfully enumerated all the charges he could make against Bottomley. He also announced that he would offer no evidence.

It was stalemate.

Mr. Justice Coleridge directed the jury to find the defendant not guilty. This meant that Bottomley had to pay the entire legal costs of the action.

But when he walked out of the court he knew the day of reckoning was fast approaching. It arrived four months later when he appeared at the Old Bailey charged with the fraudulent conversion of the Victory Bond Club's funds.

The trial was an eight-day sensation. The man whom millions had looked up to as a rather special human being was exposed as a shabby confidence trickster capable of robbing the poorest classes in the community.

This time Marshall Hall was not defending. Horatio Bottomley, in his hour of greatest need, relied upon his own skills as lay lawyer and spellbinding orator. The man who prosecuted him was the lean Travers Humphreys, who must have looked to the fleshy Bottomley a true figure of doom. Besides being a brilliant barrister, the chief prosecutor was a chartered accountant. He allowed no one in court, for more than a full week, to lose sight of the basic purpose of the prosecution. He rammed figures at the frowning jury as though they were tangible pieces of evidence that could be handled by them.

He showed how more than eighty thousand pounds had been appropriated in the defendant's name on one occasion, how a sum in excess of ten thousand pounds had been used to pay personal debts, while the famous racing stable with Bottomley's familiar colors had absorbed another fifteen thousand pounds. The story of the publicity parade with the *Deutschland* received a fresh airing, this time with a very different emphasis for the man in the street. The indictment included an additional sum of five thousand pounds paid to Bottomley's racing manager as well as five hundred to his wine merchant for champagne.

There were twenty-four counts in the indictment. Travers Humphreys made them sound like several times that number. But the heavy armament of the prosecution did not demoralize the man who knew he was fighting for his life and was prepared to say so in the witness box. Horatio Bottomley revealed a resilience and nerve that won the admiration of men who deemed him an arch-fraud.

His real chance came when he addressed the jury, and he made the most of it in the old-time tub-thumping style of the man who had covered the country making patriotic speeches to bring men to join the colors in the first years of the war.

He told them: "You have got to find that Horatio Bottomley, editor of *John Bull*, member of Parliament, the man who wrote and spoke throughout the war with the sole object of inspiring the troops and keeping up the morale of the country, who went to the front to do his best to cheer the lads—you have got to find that that man intended to steal their money. God forbid!"

At that point, to stress his reference to the Deity, he burst into tears. It was a fine histrionic performance that made his hearers with legal training squirm. Just possibly some of the jury squirmed also, but they sat stoically through the production Bottomley was making of his personal, man-to-man appeal.

After the sobbing came more flashing glances and further declamation.

"The jury has not been born that would convict me on this evidence," he asserted, trying to win the jury by a show of complete confidence in them.

He turned dramatically and stuck out a forefinger towards the sword of justice where it was hung over the judge's seat.

"That sword," he told the jury, "would fall from its scabbard if you gave a verdict of guilty against me."

As he finished speaking the words, it must have occurred to him that the jury were not looking as responsive as he could have hoped, and the sword of justice hung firmly fixed in its elevated position.

Somehow the old tricks of speech, the former antics, the well-tried clichés and solid-sounding phrases with little real meaning were not achieving expected results. The more Bottomley continued the more the wartime hero was exchanging his role for that of a mountebank. Reporters were taking down every word.

His words became a partial mumble, as though the effort was beginning to tell, but his voice cleared and the rounded phrases came again.

"I say that to you with a conscience as clear as a conscience may be . . ." and then the mumble returned.

The heat in the man was dying. He knew with growing certainty that the days of the old charm were gone, like the charm itself.

When he had finished he was sweating and exhausted. That effort had been the greatest ordeal of his life.

It was not over, however, as he discovered when Travers Humphreys' lean shape rose to its feet and the telling sardonic tone of the chief prosecutor made itself heard across the courtroom. That was a memorable occasion in the Old Bailey's long history of dramatic scenes.

A week-end intervened to destroy any lingering magic that might have clung to Bottomley's words.

When Mr. Justice Clavell-Salter finally began his summing up he spoke in a dry, emotionless voice that amply justified his nickname among admiring associates of Drysalter. As soon as the prisoner heard the judge's opening remarks he knew that the summing up would go against him, and indeed Mr. Justice Clavell-Salter seemed most anxious that the jury should understand the man being tried was not an uneducated adventurer who knew nothing about company law and corporate business procedures, but someone who was, in the judge's words, "a very able and efficient business man who had received important sums of money from people who trusted him."

When at length the jury left to consider their verdict they did not take long. Within half-an-hour they were filing back into their places. A silent court heard their finding.

"Guilty."

Bottomley was seen to stagger as he heard the word. His pudgy hands grasped the edge of the dock as though for needed support. Mr. Justice Clavell-Salter's dry tones began once more, this time addressing the prisoner and telling him of his series of heartless frauds. Bottomley, his eyes almost closed, heard the man who was about to sentence him say: "These poor people trusted you and you robbed them of a hundred and fifty thousand pounds in ten months. The crime is aggravated by your high position, by the number and poverty of your victims, by the trust they reposed in you."

There was no hint of mercy for the convicted man in that denunciatory voice. The Larceny Act of 1916, only six years earlier, stipulated that the maximum penalty for fraudulent conversion should be seven years' penal servitude. That was the sentence passed on Horatio Bottomley.

In the fullness of time Mr. Justice Hawkins had been proved a true prophet in a court that had known him very well.

THE INCREDIBLE INCENDIARIES

In the decade that passed after an Old Bailey jury had found Horatio Bottomley guilty on twenty-three counts out of twenty-four, no criminal trial caused greater excitement and interest on the part of the general public than the trial of the notorious incendiaries who made up the Leopold Harris gang.

They were unique in criminal history.

They operated against encouraging statistics. In London in the late nineteen-twenties there were six thousand fires a year that were classified by the authorities as serious. Lost in that number, for several years, were the fires specially staged by Leopold Harris and his partners in crime.

It was a thriving piece of roguery while it lasted, and it netted the gang many thousands of pounds for little work but a cold display of nerve. The incendiaries feared only one enemy, the Salvage Corps that was responsible to the insurance companies accepting fire risks. As long as the members of the Salvage Corps, who operated closely with the various fire brigades, could be hoodwinked, the gang considered itself safe.

Unfortunately for the incendiaries they had another enemy. This was a single dedicated man who was determined to prove that his suspicions were true, and that a great conspiracy to cheat the insurance companies was in being and operating with considerable success.

102

The individual was William Charles Crocker, a lawyer with a firm in Gracechurch Street, in the City of London. In the course of normal business he came to represent and act for several large insurance companies. When such companies had to pay out compensation for numbers of fires throughout the country, William Crocker undertook to investigate claims which seemed unreasonably high. His investigations led him to keep very detailed records of large fires and the claims made because of them.

Thus it was in the normal way of business that he first came to appreciate the activity of a firm of insurance assessors with a speciality in dealing with burglary and fire claims and an address in Wilson Street, one of the warren-like thoroughfares behind Finsbury Square. The firm was called Harris and Company, and had a reputable history as assessors for insurance claims. The head of the firm was a certain Leopold Harris, the son of the founder who had built up the firm's reputation. Under the aegis of the founder's son the firm moved from Wilson Street to Ropemaker Street, only a short distance away on the western side of Moorgate, and then began what William Crocker considered a marked change in policy for the firm. It began to give particular attention to fire claims, and almost invariably the claim submitted on behalf of a client was for a maximum sum, sometimes representing an inflated figure for the actual assets destroyed. But the firm of Harris and Company, under the shrewd direction of Leopold Harris, enjoyed a very marked success in bringing insurance companies to meet their claims, and from what the interested lawyer could discover, this success was due in large part to the firm's uncanny ability to be available as soon as a major fire had broken out or been reported.

The firm had a long list of satisfied clients, and their reputation for dealing expeditiously and strenuously with the unfortunate insurance companies won them additional clients. It almost appeared that Harris and Company were gaining a monopoly in their own specialist field.

This was something William Crocker viewed with mounting suspicion, especially when his compiled statistics revealed that Harris and Company had reached a stage where they were handling more fire assessments than all their competitors grouped together. The commission charged by the firm was a flat five per cent. On the volume of business they were receiving annually, the profits were mounting steadily.

When William Crocker informed his own insurance company clients of his findings, more opposition was offered to the claims submitted by Harris and Company, and on a number of occasions the claims were adjusted in favor of the companies for whom the firm of W. C. Crocker acted. But these contested claims were in a minority, and with business still booming Harris and Company were enjoying ever greater prosperity. For more than two years William Crocker continued watching the methods and results of Harris and Company without allowing the head of that firm to realize he was a subject for interested study. It was not until early in 1931 that Crocker received information of an unexpected and unusual kind.

His informant was a clerk employed by Lloyd's. This man had a friend named Cornock, who knew a certain Harry Priest, a man who claimed to be part-owner of a Stoke Newington warehouse. During a conversation in Priest's favorite hostelry, the Highbury Tavern, Cornock had been told that Priest knew where he could acquire five thousand pounds for opening a new business enterprise. Cornock had shown interest, but had not been too keen to learn the details.

These had been supplied later by the rather pressing Harry Priest, who told Cornock that the money could be obtained from a man who was known in certain quarters as the Prince. This unknown was really the head of a clever gang of operators who were expert arsonists. The gang were able to operate on a really large scale.

When Cornock manifested interest in this revelation, Priest became more confidential in tone and openly associated himself with the incendiaries. He admitted they were always on the lookout for what he called new business, which was why he had mentioned the idea of a new company to Cornock. The company would be a commercial dummy. Its stock would be almost worthless, but heavily insured. After the company had been insured for some months it would have its premises gutted by fire and its stock utterly destroyed.

Cornock wasn't sure how much of this saloon confidence was merely that of a man showing off to impress a listener. He professed to be sceptical at fooling an insurance company in this way.

"So long as you're not in their bad books, it's easy," Priest assured him. "Listen, I'll prove it."

He went on to tell Cornock that within a short time a fire would be reported in the newspapers at a certain London address in Poland Street, off Oxford Street.

The clerk from Lloyd's who had heard his friend Cornock's rather incredible story gave William Crocker the Poland Street address. The solicitor checked it and found the premises were a shop selling antiques. Daily he perused the newspapers for a report on a fire at that address. He had to wait several weeks, until he read of a fire that had gutted premises in Poland Street. The date was June 1, 1931. The gutted premises were those of the antiques shop.

The lawyer was amazed, but he now knew that his former suspicions were strongly founded. He made it his business to discover the name of the fire assessor who submitted a claim for the Poland Street fire.

The fire assessor was Leopold Harris of Harris and Company. Harris had been acting for the owner of the antiques shop, a man named Felix Bergolz. On this man's behalf Harris had submitted a claim for £5,863, of which the principal item had been a collection of Venetian glass specially insured for £4,600, which had been completely destroyed.

When William Crocker called on the general manager of the insurance company that had received the claim, he was introduced to members of Lloyd's committee, and it was agreed that funds should be made available for the lawyer's further investigation, which would continue in secret.

In the meantime Leopold Harris received a shock. The Poland Street claim was rejected *in toto*. Harris settled down to give the insurance company a fight, which was just what was required of him. The company used delaying tactics while William Crocker continued his behind-the-scenes investigation. He started with the garrulous Harry Priest, who was shadowed by relays of followers, one of whom was William Crocker's daughter. A faked car accident was staged outside Priest's warehouse. This provided an acceptable reason for claims men to appear and measure distances in the road and on the pavement, and when Harry Priest appeared in his doorway he was photographed without his knowing.

The photograph helped in establishing a connection between the part-owner of the Stoke Newington warehouse and a certain silk merchant named Camillo Capsoni, who was a partner in the Franco-Italian Silk Company, which had a Stoke Newington address. The other partner's identity was not disclosed because he had a stand-in named Harry Priest.

However, after checking back on the Franco-Italian Silk Company, William Crocker discovered with considerable interest that it was an offshoot from another firm which had operated from 185 Oxford Street eighteen months before, at the end of 1929. That company had come to a fiery end when the premises were gutted in May 1930. Camillo Capsoni had been paid twenty-two thousand pounds in insurance compensation after his claim had been submitted by Leopold Harris.

The head of Harris and Company was now fully implicated in some distinctly dubious practices. However, proof still had to be obtained—if that were possible. If it was not, then Leopold Harris could not be charged with any crime.

The investigation being made by William Crocker continued in secret, helped by a number of private detectives, for it was felt that it would be safe to go to the police only when rock-firm evidence had been obtained; otherwise Harris and his operators might find means of covering their tracks and vanishing.

For the first time, William Crocker had to consider the possibility of a large-scale conspiracy. He attempted to gauge the size of it by instituting a painstaking examination through various insurance companies and Lloyd's underwriters of past claims made by Harris and Company.

There were found to be hundreds. Surprisingly quite a few were based on conflagrations that had occurred outside London. The scope of the investigation was accordingly widened. A number of recent fires claimed special attention. For instance, just before Christmas 1930 the basement of the premises at 37 Barbican, in the City of London, was burned out while the floors above were badly damaged by the flames. This was another instance where Harris had submitted claims, on behalf of a man named Marks who ran the United Cigar and Tobacco Company, and another named Westwood, who ran a radio business. Harris secured about five thousand pounds for them from insurance claims.

Six months later, in the summer of 1931, the owner of 37 Barbican was Leopold Harris.

A claim of interest made outside London concerned a fire at 27 Dean Street, Manchester, premises housing two businesses concerned as much with silk as Camillo Capsoni. One was Richard Glen and Company, the other Acevose Silks. The address was not unfamiliar to William Crocker, nor was the name Richard Glen, for the London lawyer had investigated the claim put forward for this company and on his advice it had been rejected. On the other hand, he now found that a claim for twenty-six thousand pounds made on behalf of Acevose Silks had been paid with no delay by an insurance company for which he himself had not undertaken an investigation.

William Crocker had been suspicious, at the time of the Dean Street claim on behalf of Richard Glen, of the firm's nominal manager, a certain Ernest Wolfe, who had been at one time employed by a fishmonger. But Ernest had a brother Simon, who was found to be a particular friend of a David Harris who was Leopold's brother. There was an even more interesting tie, the lawyer discovered, when he established that in the first months of 1929 a London firm selling women's coats, Alfred Alton and Company, opened a Northern branch in Lever Street, Manchester. The stock of the Manchester branch had been destroyed in a fire not many months after it had been opened. A claim for nine thousand pounds had been submitted by Harris and had been paid. There had been a wrangle about the winding up of the firm, and the assets had been purchased at a nominal figure by Simon Wolfe for cash. Ernest's brother was a small-time furrier who would hardly have been able to find the sum required at short notice. This suggested the sum had been available in order to avoid liquidation proceedings being started, which could have been dangerous to any conspiracy.

Who had made the sum available?

One name suggested itself—Leopold Harris.

Another item struck William Crocker forcefully. He was now able to ascertain that Harris himself had been in Dean Street, Manchester, before the fire at No. 27 had been declared extinguished by the firemen. The investigating lawyer began to look for similar coincidences, and did not have to look far.

There was one in Manchester in 1927. In that year there had

been a very destructive fire at 196 Deansgate, and the premises occupied by Fabriques de Soieries, Ltd., were gutted. Another firm of silk merchants! Possibly the fancy name encouraged a fancy insurance figure of forty thousand pounds, with a further figure of half that sum to compensate for possible loss of profits in the event of fire.

Anyway, the fire that destroyed a large collection of bales of artificial silk on November 7 was still being hosed by the firemen when a man drove up from a local hotel where he had taken a room overnight and had hired a taxi. He had a companion, one of the directors of Fabriques de Soieries. The man who had hired the taxi was Leopold Harris.

The claim he had put in for the firm had been settled, after some argument, for twenty-nine thousand pounds.

The case became even more interesting when William Crocker uncovered the identity of the man who looked and spoke like an Italian when he left the taxi with Harris. His name was Camillo Capsoni.

The lawyer did not finish his inquiry into the characters concerned in this fire, and their background, until he had learned something else of eye-raising interest. This was the identity of Capsoni's fellow director in Fabriques de Soieries. He was a certain Louis Jarvis, who had earlier changed his surname from Jacobs. William Crocker proved that Jarvis was well known to Harris and that, upon one occasion, he had put in a fire claim of his own for a separate fire. The claim had gone through Leopold Harris.

The inquiry being conducted by William Crocker and his teams of private detectives now began to link up other names with those already known, and various patterns of association began to emerge in a quite alarming manner. For instance, a radio firm went up in flames in Wembley in 1931. Harris had a majority holding of shares, but other shareholders were Harry Priest and a printer named Leonard Riley, whose stock had been secured for him by that same Marks who had suffered a disastrous fire and enjoyed a successful claim at 37 Barbican. Another link up was with Art Publishers, Ltd., a firm in Accrington that employed Riley. That firm had been destroyed by fire in 1929, and Harris had secured payment of a claim for thirty thousand pounds. However, it had been too much of a coincidence when fire history repeated itself three years later and Harris claimed twenty-eight thousand pounds. Riley had been told bluntly by the local assessor that the fire had been deliberately started. That was one claim not pressed.

But the pattern had been established. Arsonists were at work, criminals who were masterminded by the man Harry Priest had said was known among the gang as the Prince.

To William Crocker the Prince was no longer an unbroken code name. He believed he had established the principal organizer of the arsonists to be Leopold Harris, known to his associates who took orders from him as the Prince.

The patient lawyer began to fill in important gaps in the pattern of criminal dealing. He checked on cases where Harris not only had a financial interest, either direct or through some proxy, but also had dealt in stock that had been supplied by a relative named Harry Gould, who claimed to be a dealer in salvaged goods, and had put in claims for some other associate who was a member of a gang with many tentacles.

The lawyer was almost ready to take what he had discovered to the police when he had a second piece of luck, the first after being contacted by the clerk from Lloyd's who had talked to Priest's drinking companion, Cornock. Camillo Capsoni quarrelled with his one-time partner in Fabriques de Soieries, Louis Jarvis. Harris was drawn into the quarrel and sided with Jarvis. The Italian was now married to a woman who, some years before, had her Continental Show Rooms in Leeds burned out. In her list of stock destroyed was a collection of Venetian glass that on paper was identical with the one supposedly destroyed later in Poland Street. It was Mrs. Capsoni who told her husband inquiries were being made and he should take steps to protect himself. She was a hard-headed Scot.

"Let me do the talking," she urged.

Her husband agreed.

Mrs. Capsoni made overtures to an insurance company that had been robbed by bogus claims, had a conference with a senior executive, claimed immunity for her husband as her price for aid, and then agreed to talk to William Crocker.

The whole story was suddenly of one gigantic and incredulous pattern. The Chief Officer of the London Salvage Corps, Captain Brynmore Eric Miles, was informed.

He appeared staggered, as well he might be, but for no reason William Crocker could guess.

Camillo Capsoni had explained how the arsonists worked by setting a wax taper upright between two celluloid photographic trays, one inside the other, and surrounding both by highly inflammable material.

When, possibly twenty minutes or more later, the lighted taper had burned down to the trays and the whole went up with a *whoosh!* the arsonist would be elsewhere establishing an alibi, should it be needed.

The fire-gang members were rounded up by Scotland Yard and in July 1933 they appeared in Number One Court at the Old Bailey before Mr. Justice Humphreys to stand trial. Roland Oliver opened the legal contest for the Crown, and when Camillo Capsoni had been called to the witness box, the prisoners' last hope of avoiding the inevitable faded.

There was no further point in clinging to a hopeful plea of not guilty. The gang's leader, Leopold Harris, turned about face and admitted to twenty-five charges of arson and fraud. His companions in the dock were shaken by this demonstration. They glanced at the judge. He seemed to be expecting a reaction from them.

They did not disappoint him.

They followed Harris in pleading guilty as they had previously followed his lead conspiring to defraud various insurance companies. In this they were possibly encouraged by an ironic observation from the Bench that co-operation by any of the accused who felt like changing their minds would earn consideration.

Only one of the gang stood pat, still pleading not guilty. That was David Harris, the friend of the ex-fishmonger's brother, Simon Wolfe. The other fifteen prisoners in the Old Bailey dock had surrendered.

Those sixteen prisoners were the largest number ever crowded into an Old Bailey dock. The trial held another record, for up to that time and for a good while afterwards it was the longest trial ever held there. It lasted six weeks. In fact, in order to bring this legal marathon to an end, Mr. Justice Humphreys went out of his way to ensure that the court sat on a Saturday so that he could pass sentence before the weekend.

His actual summing up lasted thirteen hours, time that took

up the greater part of three successive days in the trial proceedings.

Quite a large section of the court was occupied by barristers wearing wigs, for each of the prisoners was represented by counsel, and in a number of cases by more than one. The floor was covered with dispatch boxes and document files, for the counsel for the Crown had been compelled to study a number of relevant documents well in excess of a hundred thousand.

It was a trial, in fact, which wore out most of those who took an active part in it. Counsel, jurors, prisoners, even the judge were exhausted by it. Indeed, it is on record that the learned judge became so overcome by fatigue at one stage in his lengthy summing up that he allowed his mind to wander and had to apologize to the jury.

"I am wrong," he told them. "I am afraid I am a little tired."

He then went on to correct himself and continue with his survey of a truly staggering indictment of conspiracy, fraud, and arson.

Two rooms in the Old Bailey had been set aside as special archives to accommodate the documents not in immediate use in court. To have those that might be wanted readily available at the shortest possible notice an internal telephone was installed connecting the courtroom with the clerks, in charge of the case's archives. The set-up worked with surprising efficiency, for within a minute of counsel picking up the receiver in court, a required document was produced and placed in his hands. For that purpose telephone engineers had produced toned-down microphones to avoid interrupting the proceedings. Their instrument was dubbed by the reporters the whispering telephone.

The judge in his summing up dealt very scathingly with the Crown's chief witness, Camillo Capsoni, who had saved his skin by turning King's Evidence against his confederates.

"In my opinion, Capsoni is more than an accomplice," said Judge Humphreys. "He is a highly dangerous criminal. He combines the charm which we are accustomed to associate with the country from which he comes with a wickedness that is entirely his own. He is that most dangerous and detestable type, a blackmailer."

He might have been describing a modern-day criminal type.

The judge told the jury: "My chief regret is that when you have delivered your verdict I shall not be able to pass upon him the sentence he richly deserves. But without him these proceedings would have been impossible. He came voluntarily to Mr. Crocker, and had there been any threat of prosecution his mouth would have been shut."

David Harris, who stood alone, was acquitted on two counts and convicted on eight others. Each of two arson counts brought him five years' imprisonment. His brother Leopold received the maximum penalty the judge could bestow—fourteen years. The other convicted gang members were given sentences ranging from six years to a few months.

There was an epilogue to the great arson trail. From Leopold Harris's impounded bank books it had been discovered that Captain Miles, the Salvage Corps chief, had been working with the gang. Leopold Harris had guaranteed a new account for him of up to a thousand pounds. Knowing discovery was imminent, the unhappy salvage chief called on William Crocker and confessed how he had aided and abetted the gang and even leaked back to them what he had been told by the lawyer in confidence. He explained his fall from grace by foolishly allowing himself to get into debt to loan sharks and others who had blackmailed him.

Captain Miles was tried at the Old Bailey before Mr. Justice Hawke. When he had been sentenced to four years' penal servitude, the curtain had been rung down on the Leopold Harris gang for the last time.

JUSTICE COMES TO NUREMBERG

 Possibly the most unique trial of the twentieth century opened on November 20, 1945, in Nuremberg. The Second World War had not long ended, and the victors were in a mood to bring to justice those they had designated war criminals. Prisoners held for trial were those charged with crimes against peace, or war crimes, or crimes against humanity. Under such heads the leaders of the fallen Nazi Party in Germany had grave charges to answer.

The indictment ran to twenty-four thousand words, nearly half the length of this book, and before the famous trial opened a great deal of preparation had to be made, chiefly in Berlin, where the representatives of the Allied Powers met to discuss preliminaries and details of procedure.

The trial was to take its place as an event in the world's history, and for this reason it was desirable that justice should be seen to be done. The men who would render justice before the eyes of the entire world were eight legal luminaries from Britain, France, the Soviet Union, and the United States of America.

The British judges chosen were Lord Justice Lawrence and Sir Norman Birkett. For France, Messieurs Donnedieu de Vabres and Le Conseiller Falco arrived in Berlin to take their seats with the tribunal that faced months of close and demanding legal work. Major-General I. T. Nikitchenko, with Colonel A. F. Volchkov, were to represent the Government and peoples of the Soviet Union,

113

while Mr. Francis Biddle and Judge John J. Parker were to represent the United States. These representatives of their countries met in the Allied Control Authority building in a city that had been largely turned to piles of rubble by the bombs of the eastward advancing Anglo-American forces and the artillery fire of the westward advancing Soviet armies.

As soon as they had foregathered with their staff and advisers, the work of making the necessary preparations for the mass trial was begun. On one point all eight judges were agreed. No time should be lost in getting the trial opened. To further this end they met not only each day of the week, but also for long hours during the week-ends, in sessions that often lasted more than twelve hours.

Procedure was important to obviate later criticism of international law being flouted. By October 18 so much procedural work had been done that the tribunal was ready to take its first important formal steps towards rendering justice. On that day the judges met in what was termed the People's Court, and before a vast assembly of the world's foremost pressmen and journalists they were formally sworn in and accepted their seats on the Bench. They then had read the lengthy indictment against the prisoners who would stand trial. The indictment was then formally presented to them by the chosen prosecutors of each of the four nations that had appointed trial judges. Before this introductory session was over, the date for holding the actual trial had been agreed and announced.

It was an occasion that must have struck all who took part in or witnessed the proceedings as one impregnated with a grim irony. For the place where the judges took their oath was that same courtroom where, only a brief twelvemonth earlier, the Nazis had put on a legal spectacular of their own. This was the occasion when a number of German generals were tried for their roles in the abortive attempt to assassinate Hitler, carried out by Colonel Klaus Schenk, Graf von Stauffenberg, at the Wolf's Lair. In a curious way the savagery meted out to the military scapegoats on that occasion was to be avenged by the victors who had destroyed Hitlerite Germany and ended a chapter of brutality that is without parallel in the history of mankind.

The judges on their tribunal bench were formally called to order by the word "Attention!" announced loudly in English, then with a French pronunciation, and repeated at greater length in Russian, *Yve ne mania!*

The wheel of retribution had made its first turn.

Presiding on that opening day in Berlin was the Soviet judge, Major-General Nikitchenko. The British Attorney-General, Sir Hartley Shawcross, was present to make his prosecutor's opening statement. It was later claimed to be a model of what such a statement should be, terse, informative, and always to the point.

Squads of interpreters were at hand to record and translate what was said. Journalists jostled cameramen. Feature writers rubbed shoulders with historians. They were all there to ensure that no word spoken at the tribunal meeting was missed or not given a place in the official records. They represented the millions of readers throughout the world who were waiting with open minds to learn how prisoners charged with hideous crimes were judged by the legal spokesmen for the victorious democracies.

No trial had ever had such a vast audience of waiting readers. On the outcome of the deliberations of men assembled in the Berlin People's Court in October 1945 would depend the final verdict of history on National Socialism and the men who had composed and created its creed of *Herrenvolk* and slave races.

By the inference democracy too was on trial, for the judges were sworn to abide by a democratic concept of both law and the rights of the individual.

The judges of the various nations would take their places alternately, and the presiding judge on each sitting would be chosen in rotation. Justice would not only be done. It would be done impartially.

When the tribunal sitting at the Berlin People's Court terminated this first important session they disbanded prior to the opening of the trial proper in Nuremberg. The English party flew back to England, transported by the R.A.F.

Behind them they left the prisoners who were to be tried in Nuremberg studying the lengthy indictment, copies of which had been served to each. Nuremberg had been chosen for the trial because it had been a city the Nazis had made their own. It was in Nuremberg that great rallies of Nazi armed might and of Nazi youth had been held in the years when the National Socialist creed was being propagated and Germany was flexing her warrior's muscles. In the vast arena where the rallies had been staged Adolf Hitler and his Party chiefs had stood to gloat over the evidence of a war machine they had created and a way of life they had forced the German people to accept. Nuremberg, like Berlin, had been largely reduced to bombed rubble, but it was a place of memories.

Those memories were to be harshly stirred when in late November the trial opened in the Court House. For a great many of them a price would be demanded. Moreover, that price would be paid. Men who had for years lived outside the concept of normal civilized law were to die when brought inside it. Even so, the price demanded was only a token payment for the misery and degradation the Nazi creed had spread like a vast stain over the world.

At ten o'clock in the morning of November 20 the stage had been set. The hundreds of thousands of statements and documents, photographs and maps, files and records, had all been docketed, translated, and indexed after being assembled as evidence for the court's consideration. Most of the official Nazi records had been removed from one-time Party and Government buildings. On the evidence afforded by them, and by those additional statements and documents that had been painstakingly collected and annotated, would hang the fate of the score of prisoners who were to take their unenviable places in the Nuremberg Court House.

Responsibility for the smooth running of the purely physical aspects of the great trial lay in the hands of the United States authorities, for Nuremberg was in the U.S. Zone of partitioned Germany. The U.S. technicians and their work must have impressed the members of the various Allied delegations. They had, for instance, incorporated in the courtroom an instantaneous translation system in the four languages of the judges and the defendants —English, French, Russian, and German. Any authorized person attending the trial was provided with a seat where he or she was given headphones and a dialling switch by means of which the evidence or statement being made to the court could be heard in any of the four languages, according to the switch used on the dial.

Outside the courtroom the corridors and passages were guarded by American soldiers who demanded sight of anyone's official pass before that person was allowed to continue. The world's interest in the proceedings, as evinced during the days at Berlin, proved to be only a foretaste of the mass global excitement created by the trial itself. It was found necessary to broadcast the opening stages of the trial. The Americans were not caught unprepared. The national talent for publicity and advertising had thought of every media in which the trial could be given to the world at large without delay and with the fullest coverage.

In the dock were the twenty men on trial. The number was less than originally counted. One, Martin Bormann, was still to be accounted for. He had not been captured, and there were reports that he was dead, but the reports had not been confirmed. Two remained in hospital, too ill to attend the hearing, while the fourth, whose name would still be heard in that court, Robert Ley, had committed suicide rather than face what he had considered inevitable.

The first entry of the international judges from the private room where they had assembled was heralded by the announcement: "The International Military Tribunal will now enter." The American soldiers spaced around the courtroom stood to attention. Prosecuting and defense counsel, prisoners in the dock, the vast concourse of reporters and photographers and privileged members of the general public rose to their feet as a dark door opened and into the courtroom filed the eight men charged with deciding the destiny of the twenty Germans watching their entry. They took their places at the long tribunal bench, behind which were draped curtains with the flags of the judges' nations raised in places of honor. Six of the judges wore sober black gowns. The two Russians wore their military uniforms. For such an international occasion the British judges were without their familiar wigs.

After the judges were seated the others present sat down. The trial was in session. It was to run for two hundred and eighty-four days, with more than four hundred open sessions.

As the proceedings opened, the eyes of most in the court glanced towards the rows of prisoners. Only one appeared alert and personable. That was Hermann Goering, the creator of the Third Reich's Luftwaffe, the World War One pilot who had taken over the command of Manfred von Richthofen's Flying Circus after their leader had been killed in action. Like his co-defendants, when it came his time to plead he took the formal German oath.

"I swear by God the Almighty the Omniscient," he said in his deep tones that occasionally became gruff, "I will speak the whole truth and will withhold nothing and add nothing."

Yet when his counsel, Dr. Otto Stahmer, called a witness to testify on the Luftwaffe leader's behalf, he chose a frowning Swede named Bergen Dahlerus, a well-known industrialist. The best the Swedish man of industry could say for Hermann Goering proved to be a further indictment of his guilt in the collective inhumanities of the Nazi Party. Goering heard the evidence stone-faced, as though he realized there would be no loophole through which his prison-thinned figure could wriggle in a legal escape.

Not so the mystery man of Nazi Germany, that same Ribbentrop who had peddled champagne and propaganda among the capitals of Europe. He was full of denials. He told the court he had known of only two concentration camps organized by the Nazis. One was at Oranenburg, the other at Dachau. The protest was revealed as an empty lie when a screen was lowered before the prisoner's gaze and on it was flashed a map drawn to scale. The center of that map was familiar to him. It was his own *Schloss* at Fuschl. Around it were thirty-three dots. Each was a known concentration camp. The man who had sworn to tell the whole truth and to withhold nothing was tongue-tied when the purport of the map was explained. A hundred thousand unfortunates had been doomed within the camps, none of which was more than eight miles from Fuschl, where champagne had flowed like water in a spring thaw.

But the screen that flashed the map for Ribbentrop's jaded memory had other striking evidence to offer. Some of the evidence, taken from the Nazis' own records, made those in court catch their breath. One such piece of evidence was a length of film taken by a Nazi official photographer after the destruction of Lidice, where an entire populace had been exterminated. Another Nazi with an unshaking hand had recorded scenes when the resistance fighters of Warsaw had been overcome. Those scenes lived again with terrible poignancy and blood-chilling starkness in the Nuremberg courtroom. The justification of the terrible indictment of war crimes against peace and humanity was not only heard in that courtroom, it was seen.

In the main, the defense of those twenty men on trial was that they had been men acting under orders. In essence those orders derived from the leader of their political party, Adolf Hitler. But Sir Hartley Shawcross dealt shortly and sharply with that concept of duty.

"It is no excuse for the common thief to say, 'I stole because

I was told to steal', for the murderer to plead, 'I killed because I was asked to kill,' " he told an attentive court, and went on, gesturing to the men in the dock, "These men are in no different position for all it was nations they sought to rob, whole peoples they tried to kill. 'The warrant of no man excuseth the doing of an illegal act,' " he reminded his listeners. "Political loyalty, military obedience are excellent things. But they neither require nor do they justify the commission of patently wicked acts. There comes a point where a man must refuse to answer to his leader if he is also to answer to his conscience."

There was no shuffling on the tribunal's bench, where the looks on the faces of the judges gave proof that those days of preliminary work, of coming to common agreement about what could be accepted and what rejected, had been time very well spent.

There were interruptions to the trial, however, and one of them occurred when the British Attorney-General had to return to England because of the pressure of his work for Parliament. But his absence did not hold up the trial proceedings, for the British prosecutor's deputy, Sir David Maxwell Fyfe, had been fully briefed about the evidence he was to present, and indeed almost the entire British prosecution of the war criminals was undertaken by him, supported by two Welshmen, Colonel Griffith-Jones and Major E. Elwyn Jones, both of whom had persuasive lilting voices. One American lawyer who heard them said to Sir Norman Birkett's clerk, "Those Jones brothers are sure easy to listen to."

Probably it made a difference where one sat in that courtroom. The translated words of the Welshmen might not have sounded so pleasant through a pair of headphones worn in the prisoners' dock.

But whatever the defendants thought of the voices of those haranguing them and questioning their acts and motives, they could have no valid complaint against the unscrupulous fairness of the trial's general procedure and of the treatment accorded men who knew they were on trial for their lives.

Any and every point of detail, whether raised by the prosecution or the defense, was meticulously considered and debated until either uncertainty or ambiguity was removed. It was a trial in which the rights of the individual were always foremost in the minds of those pursuing the prosecution. All this was contrived despite language barriers and variations of precise legal concepts. It was a great triumph for rational and right thinking.

Whatever the trial's outcome, throughout those two hundred and eighty-four difficult days of conscientious prosecution, the great standard of utter fairness in the presentation of testimony and trial exhibits was maintained. Indeed, the Nuremberg trial set an international standard the world has several times since tried to achieve without success.

It not only provided defendants with an object lesson in impartiality and fairness, it gave a number of striking contrasts which made their own impact on the tireless listeners. The French prosecutors, led by the formidable Maître Auguste Champetier de Ribes, were nimble and quick off the mark, making their points and scoring with devastating legal dexterity. They were angry men keeping a tight rein on themselves. They strove to be faultless and they succeeded.

As did the Soviet prosecuting counsel. Like the Soviet tribunal judges, they wore their Service uniforms. They were very different in temperament from their Allied colleagues. They seemed to be more plodding in the development of their case, and behaved like men with no thought for time, only for what they had to do. But occasionally anger broke through their rigid control of personal feelings. It was never more than a flash. But always it was something felt in that courtroom where in the winter days the lights burned for long hours and sometimes men's breath made little clouds before their frowning faces.

The American prosecution team was also a formidable one, led by a rugged colonel named Amen, who had a distinctive way of adopting a challenging pose towards witnesses he questioned. Perhaps he had taken his cue from the peroration of his compatriot, Mr. Justice Jackson, who was to lay bare the sham defense in the name of duty when he addressed the judges.

"The flowering of this system," said the American speaker, "is represented in the fanatical SS General Ohlendorf, who told this tribunal without shame or trace of pity how he personally directed the putting to death of ninety thousand men, women, and children. They developed a contest in crime and cruelty. Ohlendorf from the witness stand accused other SS commanders, whose killings exceeded his own, of exaggerating their figures."

Mr. Justice Jackson went on: "The Nazi despotism does not consist of these individual defendants alone. A thousand little Führers dictated; a thousand imitation Goerings strutted; a thousand von Schirachs incited the youth; a thousand Saukels worked the slaves; a thousand Streichers and Rosenbergs stirred up hatred against the Jews; a thousand Kaltenbrunners and Franks tortured and killed; and a thousand Schachts, Speers, and Funks administered and financed this movement."

His listeners were left in no doubt as to the wider implications of the trial of the twenty in the dock.

He went on: "It is important that this trial should not serve to absolve the whole German people except the twenty in the dock. Their power is finished, and no more can they lead their misguided followers to destruction. But we do not allow their assistants to slide out without any attempt to lay them by the heels."

In those words was the promise of the war criminal trials that were to follow throughout the years ahead. He went on to put some unsettling rhetorical questions.

"How did these few men who were the heads of the Nazi regime," he asked, "kill five million Jews, as they boast they did? They did not do it with their hands. It took disciplined, organized, systematic human manpower to do it. It was organized, directed, and used. How can the killing of five million people be a secret? Were not the concentration camps known in every one of our countries? Wasn't it a byword in every land in the world—the German concentration camp? And yet we have to sit here patiently and listen to arguments that the German people had no knowledge of it."

After a dramatic pause he said sternly: "We do not desire the deaths of millions of Germans. Had we done so we were not short of shells, guns, and tanks when we accepted their unconditional surrender. We could have gone on and done it then, had we so desired."

A glance at the men in the dock at that moment during the trial would have found them looking like prophets of their own doom. The fact that the German nation was also being held accountable for crimes committed in its name and by its accepted and acknowledged leaders did nothing to sweeten the personal bitterness of the defendants.

However, the progress of the trial was not accomplished smoothly without the collection of international judges often requiring closed sessions in their own conference room. In such sessions and during the open sessions in the courtroom, the man who sat next to the Soviet judges was Sir Norman Birkett. Several observers from both in court and behind the scenes have made the point that the English judge was responsible several times for clearing up threatened differences of opinion with his Russian co-judges. What was said in the closed sessions remains secret, but they effectively cleared away doubts that rose naturally through the subtleties of language and the interpretation of agreed rules by variously trained minds. Nothing was allowed to interrupt the general progress of the trial. It continued remorselessly. Through winter, spring, and summer. For nearly three hundred days the world received a daily portion of trial evidence and testimony that made it shiver or feel numbed with shock, so that when at last the great trial was over it was hard for many people to believe justice had been served fully.

The sentences, when they were announced, had a puny quality when set beside the figures of millions exterminated.

Of the twenty who had sat throughout the trial in the Nuremberg dock, eleven were sentenced to death after being found guilty as charged. The sentence was to be carried out by hanging, the death universally accorded to felons guilty of a capital crime. The absent Bormann was another sentenced to death.

Of the remaining nine, three were sentenced to life imprisonment while others received varying terms of twenty, fifteen, and ten years' imprisonment.

Three of those indicted were found not guilty of the crimes with which they were charged and were duly acquitted by the Allied tribunal. These three were Schacht the banker, Von Papen the diplomat, another mystery man among the Nazis, and the straitlaced General Fritzsche.

So that truly justice was observed to be done in Nuremberg. More than that, a model had been established for the future trials of arrested war criminals, and this was by no means the least important outcome of the famous trial.

In the years ahead there would be no Allied tribunal of selected judges to try those charged with war crimes. The prisoners would be tried by German courts with German judges. Just how the temper of the German people had changed since the days of Adolf Hitler and the Nuremberg trial was demonstrated when a wanted war criminal named Martin Sommer was unmasked and brought to trial in the summer of 1958.

He had been the brutal camp commandant at Buchenwald, where thousands had died. His trial was staged in Munich. It was given world-wide publicity.

Martin Sommer was found guilty and sentenced by a court of his fellow-countrymen to life imprisonment.

The Nuremberg kind of justice was still seen to be making its impact in the land where once justice had been a word with which to threaten the innocent.

THE DOUBLE BETRAYAL

Not all famous trials have a spectacular quality. Indeed, the trials that proceeded from the arrests of the notorious atomic spies, Alan Nunn May and Klaus Fuchs, were somewhat in the nature of an anti-climax to the work involved in bringing men branded as traitors to justice.

The story of Fuchs possibly made the greater impact because it came as a kind of sorry sequel to the tale of Nunn May, three years after the latter had gone to prison.

It was during that momentous year of 1945 that saw the end of the Second World War and the opening of the Nuremberg War Crimes Trial, as it had been labelled, that a clerk at the Soviet embassy in Ottawa who deciphered codes walked out on his job and his employers and took with him the code book he had used in his work and some recently received telegrams for dispatch to Moscow. The information in the telegrams he had been given to code concerned Soviet espionage operations within Canada.

Igor Gouzenko, the defecting cipher clerk, hoped to be able to buy immunity from arrest and possible safety from the secret police of his own country with the code book and telegrams. He was not the first turncoat, however, to discover that his self-adopted role did not inspire confidence in those with whom he wished to trade. Indeed, Gouzenko found the market for a spy's wares a difficult one to break into. A number of people he approached gave him to understand they didn't wish to be involved or else they openly discredited his wares.

Afraid of being discovered as a traitor by his superiors, and aware that time was not a commodity of which he had any great stock, he approached the editor of a newspaper when almost in despair. However, the hard heads in the editorial room of the *Ottawa Journal* soon showed him the door into the street. By this time Gouzenko decided he required support. He returned the next day with his wife. He did his best to establish his identity in the newspaper office. Perhaps in this he was successful, but he failed to make progress. Again he was shown the door, his wife with him.

The next stage in the Gouzenko affair came close to being outright farce. The despairing cipher clerk returned home to find a couple of tough characters whom he recognized as Soviet secret police searching through his apartment. That meant finding cover in a hurry and if it was not too late. Gouzenko sought sanctuary from a neighbor he knew who was a sergeant in the Royal Canadian Air Force. The neighbor was startled by the Russian's disclosure. Being a man of action, he left Gouzenko in his flat and went off to get the Ottawa police interested in what he had been told.

The sergeant had better luck than Gouzenko with the story he had to tell. The Ottawa police were soon turning the Soviet secret police out of an apartment where they did not belong. They locked the door and kept the key. They also kept Igor Gouzenko as well as his code book and sheafs of telegrams in Russian.

The Royal Canadian Mounted Police were contacted and they took over from the Ottawa local detectives. When they questioned the man now being held in protective custody they quickly realized the value of the documents he had brought with him from the office in the Soviet embassy where Colonel Zabotin's word was law.

The colonel was revealed as the man responsible for the direction of a vast Soviet spy network in Canada that had tributaries extending into the United States. Indeed, Zabotin was revealed as a dangerous spy-master in regular contact with the Moscow headquarters referred to as The Centre. It was to The Centre that the telegrams Gouzenko had filched had been directed.

The telegrams and other helpful documents that had been stuffed into the code book gave the Canadian authorities sufficient information to reveal the identities of most of Zabotin's North American contacts, both in Canada and in the United States. This was the exclusive spy scoop of the century that the over-cautious editorial men on the staff of the *Ottawa Journal* had turned down.

Some of the contacts named had obvious code names and one of these was Alek, who seemed to be an important cog in a whirling wheel of devious espionage. Questioned about Alek, Gouzenko admitted that he did not know the man's real identity. He knew him only by his code name. However, establishing Alek's identity was not likely to be very difficult if one was patient, for a telegram in the collection produced by the cipher clerk stated that Alek was on the point of returning to England.

This apparently established him as an Englishman.

Another telegram mentioned that Alek would be, after his return, working at King's College of the University of London. A very different kind of telegram was sent to Scotland Yard, who made a number of inquiries. It was checked that there was only one Britisher about to return to England from Canada to work at King's College, London. He was a scientist, and his name was Alun Nunn May.

This proved to be truly alarming. For Alan Nunn May had been engaged on secret work in the United States. Yet this man was known to the Russians in North America as Alek. It looked very much as though Nunn May was a man who should not be trusted with secrets.

Inquiries were made about him and his background was filled in. Nunn May was born in 1912 and at school revealed a preference for science subjects. He eventually went to Cambridge, where he was an undergraduate at Trinity. He became a physicist and during the Second World War had been employed in the university's Cavendish laboratories on some top-secret research. The work had been given the name of Tube Alloy Project, which was far from being a helpful description.

Some time later in the war, in July 1944, Dr. Cockcroft, the Jacksonian Professor of Natural Philosophy, was appointed the director of the Atomic Energy Project at Montreal and Chalk River, in Canada, and when he left Cambridge to take up his new post he invited Nunn May, with a number of other young Cambridge scientists, to join him.

Alan Nunn May had accepted, but his acceptance had actually come from Canada, where he had gone in January 1943 with other British scientists to work under Dr. Halban, who had at one time worked with Professor Joliot-Curie, the French specialist in radium research.

At this point the probing into Nunn May's background was helped by one of the Gouzenko telegrams, for the reference to Alek, now suspected of being Nunn May, indicated that Alek had been recruited as a Communist agent. But not by Colonel Zabotin. By The Centre in Moscow. It was from The Centre that Zabotin had received instructions to make contact with Alek and include him in the organization working from the office of the man who was ostensibly the Soviet military attaché in Ottawa. For this to be the case it was obvious that Nunn May was known to Moscow. To be known to Moscow he must have been a secret member of the Communist Party in Britain.

The research into Nunn May's background became a three-way detective project, with the American FBI involved. It was established that from late September until late October 1944 the man who had joined the Cockcroft research project from Canada had been working with American scientists on a very secret piece of research with the code name of Manhattan District Project. For this vital month he had lived on the premises of the Argonne laboratory in Chicago. It was the fourth visit Nunn May had made to America. When a fifth visit was suggested, the director of the Manhattan District Project, Major General Leslie R. Groves, refused to give his consent to the proposal. At the time he kept his reasons to himself, but later he admitted that, in his opinion, Nunn May was being given too great an opportunity to appreciate the direction the later developments of Manhattan District Project was taking.

But his natural wariness was too late to help safeguard his secret project.

It was on August 9, 1945, forty-eight hours after an American plane had atom-bombed Hiroshima, that Colonel Nikolai Zabotin telegraphed in code to The Centre the particulars of American production of Uranium 235 at Oak Ridge in the Tennessee Valley and at the Hanford Engineering Works, which is on the Columbia River in the State of Washington. There was some important additional information. This was that the Hiroshima bomb was made with Uranium 235, and that he had received a sample of it—supplied by Alek.

There was now no doubt as to the weight of evidence provided by the defecting cipher clerk in Ottawa. Dr. Alan Nunn May had been a spy for the Russians. He had not only supplied them with information, but with material for their own scientists to work on.

Information from yet another of the telegrams told Scotland Yard that Nunn May was being directed to make contact with a Soviet agent in London. The meeting would take place at eight o'clock in the evening in Great Russell Street. Nunn May, or Alek as he was still called by both Moscow and Zabotin, was to appear at that hour outside the entrance to the closed British Museum. He would carry in his hand a copy of that day's *Times*. His contact would approach with a distinctive copy of *Picture Post*, a weekly illustrated journal of the time, in his hand.

The contact would speak first.

He would stop and ask the man carrying the *Times*, "What's the shortest way to the Strand?"

Alek's response was to be, "Come along. I'm going that way."

However, just in case coincidence should be wrecking a carefully prepared spy rendezvous, Alek was to say shortly after falling into step with the other man carrying *Picture Post*, "Best regards from Mike!"

A series of dates were supplied for the meeting in Great Russell Street. Any evening in October with a seven it it—i.e., the 7th, 17th, or 27th. If those dates were impossible they were to be repeated in November, and if these too proved impossible to keep the same dates should be kept in December.

Preparations were made by Commander Leonard Burt and Superintendent Spooner of the Special Branch to observe the secret meeting between Nunn May and his new contact. They rented a room in Great Russell Street which gave them a wide-angle view of the approach to the entrance of the British Museum, and on nine separate occasions over three months with the weather becoming steadily colder they kept their own secret vigil. All to no purpose.

Nunn May did not appear outside the British Museum at the appointed hour on any of the listed dates. That brought the Yard men to the end of the road they had been travelling. It wasn't difficult to realize that, after the defection of Igor Gouzenko, The Centre had taken steps to have Nunn May warned not to obey the instructions he had received. But how the Russian embassy in London had contrived this, Commander Burt could not be sure. He had had Nunn May followed daily by a squad of detectives and the scientist's telephone had been tapped.

It was now 1946. Burt waited for January to pass and then made an appointment to see Nunn May in his office at Shell-Mex House in the Strand, not a great distance from King's College. It was no more than making contact. Burt did not put any awkward questions, and the scientist in no way betrayed his actions or feelings. He remained quite calm and sure of himself. Burt did not remain long.

However, within a short time of making this visit fresh information from Canada suggested that there should be no further delay in arresting the man who had supplied Soviet Russia with a valuable sample of Uranium 235. For one thing, the Canadian Prime Minister, Mackenzie King, had announced to the Press the known existence of a Soviet spy ring in Canada and he disclosed that thirteen agents had been arrested.

A return visit to Shell-Mex House was arranged five days after the first. This time it was a very different Nunn May who received the two Yard men. He was nervous when he opened the door to his visitors, and his nervousness only increased when Burt lost no time in telling the scientist that he understood Nunn May should have made contact with a Soviet agent outside the British Museum, but that he had not kept the appointment.

Nunn May tried to put up a bluff, saying he did not know what the other was implying.

At that, Commander Burt told him what he knew.

Alan Nunn May dropped into a chair and covered his face with his hands, as though he needed a few moments of privacy from the quizzical quality of the Yard men's eyes. He would have been better employed rubbing the scales from his own eyes. Nunn May had reached the end of the traitor's path he had trod. He was about to be exposed for the secret role he had elected to play in helping a potential enemy of his country.

Some while later he made a statement. It was written out at his dictation by Spooner. In it he said: "I gave and had given very careful consideration to the correctness of making sure that the development of atomic energy was not confined to the U.S.A. I took the painful decision that it was necessary to convey general information on atomic energy and make sure it was taken seriously."

There could be only one motive urging the man who made that calculated statement. He was a man who felt a greater allegiance to the Soviet Union than to his own country, and for ideological reasons. He had done a great deal more than convey general information. He had provided purloined material that had put Soviet scientists years ahead of their own research at the time they received it. What Nunn May had done was to save Soviet researchers years of wasted effort and to put them on the road to catching up with the American and British atomic scientists.

In doing this he threatened to turn the cold war into a series of admitted hostilities with a much warmer climate. He put a rift in American-Soviet relations that is still obvious today.

At least he had not sought monetary gain for his traitorous conduct. In return for information and concrete proof worth a vast sum in roubles he had received some seven hundred dollars to defray expenses and two bottles of whisky. Not even vodka!

In his full statement he went out of his way not to implicate Soviet embassy officials in Canada or any Communist Party members. This was not the ingenuous care for truth that he sought to suggest. It was the careful training of the spy who had been well briefed and had received implicit instructions on how to behave in certain eventualities.

In short, the more one understands his actions, the more one loses a sneaking sympathy with Nunn May the scientist having trouble with his conscience, and discovers a contempt for Nunn May the man who betrayed his friends and colleagues and those who had mistakenly put their trust in his integrity as a man.

He was duly charged under the Official Secrets Act, and his trial opened at the Central Criminal Court in London in the month after his arrest.

It was a trial without fireworks. In fact, it proved to be something of a disappointment to the many readers of national newspapers who had expected startling developments. For one thing, the prisoner pleaded guilty to the charge, which was the guarded one of having "communicated information to unauthorized persons." The trial, in effect, was staged to give nothing away. Nunn May had completed his usefulness to both friends and enemies. His somewhat disappointing trial was famous because of what was not allowed to be said during the proceedings. But it was also famous for another reason.

It marked a notable milestone in the twentieth century. The first atomic spy had been unmasked and revealed as a new species of traitor to be given consideration and study in an age when men's loyalties were being pressured into new shapes and when conscience was being given a new definition.

Dr. Alan Nunn May was only the first of several atomic spies and scientist traitors who came on trial in the post-war years. The second to achieve notoriety was Dr. Klaus Fuchs. His name became known widely after most people had tried to forget Nunn May's.

Nunn May's access to top secret nuclear information was a direct result of faulty screening by British security officials. They had not discovered that he had joined the Communist Party nor that he even had Communist sympathies, much less owed allegiance to the Soviet Union.

For this oversight, British security methods became suspect in the eyes of the Americans. Three years after Nunn May went to prison they became even more suspect.

The reason was a bad slip by a Soviet delegate at a conference held by the United Nations Atomic Energy Commission. He may have been full of vodka or he may have been a naïve person who should never have been allowed to occupy the position he did. Anyway, whatever the reason, he became boastful. He informed the commission members that the Soviet Union had acquired atomic information which the United States did not believe anyone else possessed.

Perhaps he realized the stupidity of such a remark once he had uttered it. If he did, it was too late to do anything about it. U.S. Intelligence was not too thin-skinned to take a badly timed taunt. But it was too well trained to overlook the obvious. There was another atomic spy at large and he had access to U.S. secret material.

Moreover, he couldn't have received what he had passed on to the Soviet Union from Nunn May, and nothing about this spy's work was referred to in the Gouzenko documents. So he was an unknown.

Within hours, the FBI were narrowing down the field of search for the hidden spy. They were left with several names of possible Soviet secret agents, but the one they favored was Klaus Fuchs, who had been passed on to America from England. Not that Fuchs was English. He was German and had escaped as a refugee to England at the time the Nazis were rounding up Communists and fellow-travellers. He too was a scientist with a brilliant potential. When war came he was readily absorbed into a team of British researchers, and he worked on projects in Glasgow and later in Birmingham, where, curiously enough, he was under the direction of another native German who was a refugee, and one whom he had known in Germany, Rudolf Peierls.

What British security failed to discover in their screening of Fuchs was that he had been a member of a secret Communist underground group of professional men. Something else they did not find out was that, since coming to England, Fuchs had been recruited for additional activities by Simon Kremer, the secretary to the Soviet military attaché in London.

Because of his capabilities as a scientist, Fuchs was another young researcher who was dispatched to the United States. He arrived in New York in December 1943, the same year Nunn May was in Canada. He was given work first at Columbia University, and later was drafted to more secret work at the atom bomb plant at Los Alamos, in New Mexico. By this time he had ceased sending monthly reports to Simon Kremer and had been passed on to the Soviet espionage network in the States to keep liaison with an American traitor named Harry Gold. That was a day Fuchs was to remember, for Gold became the means of the Americans finding him after the verbal bomb had exploded at the meeting of the United Nations Atomic Energy Commission.

Fuchs must have thought himself safe enough when he returned to England in 1946, after the close of hostilities, with a post promised him at the Harwell Establishment. Contact with the Soviet spy network in Britain was renewed and once more Fuchs began handing over regular reports on his work and what he could learn about the work of fellow-scientists.

However, in Fuchs's case, ironically, it was the scientist who began to have a change of heart about the masters he served. World events were opening his eyes to the real nature of certain Soviet activities and these produced doubts in his mind and an increasing desire to cut adrift. He stopped keeping appointments and failed to hand over reports. He was a man suddenly afraid of his one-time masters and became a prisoner in his own mental cage, fearful of trying to escape from the only world he knew—the Atomic Energy Establishment at Harwell.

But while he was lying low the FBI was probing a network of suspects in the States, and eventually they were led to discover Harry Gold and his activities on behalf of the Soviet spy ring in North America.

Gold was clever. He managed to turn the FBI operatives' attention away from the direction where the truth lay. He kept them watching himself. As long as he did that, Klaus Fuchs and his former activities were a safe secret.

But Gold was at best an amateur. The time came when he contradicted himself, and that was a bad mistake to make. It meant the FBI went back to the beginning and started checking his story again. This time they came up with a different answer. It not only implicated Gold. It pointed to Klaus Fuchs.

Fuchs had supplied Gold with important classified material about the work undertaken at Los Alamos. Gold had passed it on. Hence the ability of the Soviet scientists to bridge the gap between the results of their research after receiving Nunn May's help and the successes obtained by the Americans.

Rocket missiles and nuclear warheads and even space ships had been brought several stages nearer to perfected reality.

The concept of an atom spy had not been limited to a single man named Nunn May. He was shown to be a new and even dedicated species of spy, a specialist stealer of other people's secrets.

So an interval had been filled in, between 1946 and 1949, when at last the FBI was able to put the British on the trail of the unknown atom spy in their midst. British security was rocked clear down to its threadbare socks by what the Americans had learned from Harry Gold. For the second time in three years it had been shown to be cruelly lacking in effective methods of screening scientists whose background at least gave room for tentative suspicion.

The Special Branch was once more handed the job of keeping tabs on a man who had come to consider himself belatedly in the clear, free of the shadow men of the Soviet Union he had served and free of the men he had betrayed.

But Klaus Fuchs was living in a fool's paradise where the atmosphere was a trifle too rare for his health. He did not realize that he was being closely watched, his every movement recorded, his post observed, his phone calls monitored. Solely because he was living in his own self-created vacuum there was nothing for the watchful Special Branch detectives to mark up against him.

It seemed that they were wasting their time.

They were not prepared to continue doing that indefinitely with Harry Gold under arrest in the United States and the whole business of Fuchs's duplicity and double-dealing very much on record.

Fuchs was approached. The appearance of detectives to ask questions he could only answer by implicating himself as a spy for the Soviet espionage network was more than Fuchs could accept with any hope of bluffing his way out of trouble. He realized that what he had most feared had happened.

His double role in America was known.

It didn't take Fuchs long to break down and confess the truth. When his version of the truth was told, it had a number of aspects that were surprising to his well-briefed listeners.

He had gone hunting his Soviet contact in New York City with a new white tennis ball in his hand, and he had been accosted by a stranger wearing an unusual style in gloves and carrying a book with a bright green cover. This stranger had kept his eyes on Fuchs's tennis ball as he hailed a taxi. They had driven to a restaurant on lower Third Avenue, where the stranger unburdened himself of his code name.

"I am Raymond."

That was the name by which Fuchs knew him throughout the period of their association. To Raymond, Fuchs explained the latest atom project known as the Manhattan Engineer District, by which fissionable uranium would be used to provide the destructive energy of a military weapon.

"Can you get details?" Raymond pressed the man who had no code name, but was known to him as Klaus Fuchs.

"Later—I think," was the guarded reply.

They finished their drinks, made arrangements for the next

meeting, and went their separate ways, Raymond to report to the Soviet espionage network, Fuchs back to New Mexico. It was early in 1944. Not long afterwards Fuchs began to pass over to Raymond details of the work being done in the Los Alamos plant. What he provided the Soviet agents through the medium of Raymond complemented and confirmed what Nunn May had provided.

It was only on January 27, 1950, that Klaus Fuchs, by this time confronted by MI5 men as well as the chief security officer at Harwell, agreed to make a statement. He had no real alternative. He had been convinced that the man he had known only as Raymond was actually the arrested Harry Gold who had talked.

After news of his arrest had been reported in the United States a spokesman for the Joint Congressional Committee on Atomic Energy stated: "It is hardly an exaggeration to say that Fuchs alone has influenced the safety of more people and accomplished greater damage than any other spy not only in the history of the United States, but in the history of nations."

He too was brought to trial at the Central Criminal Court, where he appeared on March 1. Like Nunn May, he pleaded guilty, in his case to providing 'to persons unknown' information calculated to be useful to an enemy.

The trial was a sequel to that held when Nunn May appeared at the Old Bailey. Fuchs's counsel, Derek Curtis-Bennett, did his best to mitigate his client's crime, and pointed out that at the time Fuchs became a British subject in 1942 "he was a known Communist, and he had never pretended he was anything else."

Listening British security officials must have squirmed very uncomfortably as the defense counsel made a point of this stale truth. They must have squirmed even more uncomfortably as counsel drove home a grim fact of life.

"Anyone who had read anything about Marxist theory," Derek Curtis-Bennett continued, "must know that a man who is a Communist, whether in Germany or Timbuctoo, will react in exactly the same way. When he gets information he will automatically and unhappily put his allegiance to the Communist idea first."

It was an explanation, but hardly to be classified as evidence in mitigation.

The trial achieved special notoriety when the frowning Lord Chief Justice addressed his own scathing remarks to the prisoner at the close of this sequel to the Nunn May trial.

L. C. J. Goddard told Fuchs, whom he was about to sentence for his crime: "You have betrayed the hospitality and protection given to you with the grossest treachery."

Those words offered a clue to the sentence about to be given the man in the dock. Fuchs braced himself.

"The maximum sentence ordained is fourteen years", said the Lord Chief Justice in even and unhurried tones. "That is the sentence I pass upon you."

In the not distant future the machinations of other atomic scientist spies were to be uncovered, and the atomic spy in turn was to give pride of place to the diplomatic spy in an age in which secret agents and undercover operators were to become an everyday reality to harassed security men throughout the entire world. The hallmark of shame reserved for those who were caught and tried had been established in the Old Bailey trials of the atomic spies, Nunn May and Klaus Fuchs.

TEENAGERS ON A ROOF

Few murder trials at the Old Bailey in the second half of the present century have evoked such public interest and concern as that which opened before Lord Goddard two weeks before Christmas 1952. In the dock were two youths charged with the murder of a policeman during a raid on a warehouse near Croydon.

Public interest was held by the stark tragedy that had been enacted on the night of the shooting. Public concern was given to the penalties the youths faced, for there was a discrepancy in their ages which meant that if both were found guilty only one could die by hanging. In law, the other was too young to be executed. Yet the prosecution claimed that it was the younger who had fired the fatal shot.

Predictably such a case aroused the fervid partisanship of the vocal abolitionists who wanted the death penalty removed from the statute book. Sociologists waxed eloquent about modern youth, reformers wanted education and social conditions changed. The Press devoted columns to every possible social aspect of the case. On radio and television publicists and personalties were insistent in keeping the public aware of the terrible pathos of the case.

Small wonder that for a space of months the names of Christopher Craig and his older friend Derek Bentley became, in the most unfortunate and unhappy way, household words in Britain.

Christopher Craig was sixteen in 1952, a youth who hero-worshipped his older brother, Nevin Scott Craig, who had been released from prison in 1950 after serving five years for armed robbery. In September 1952 the older brother was arrested in North London by police officers who raided the house where he slept with a gun under his pillow. He was charged with taking part in a robbery at Waltham Abbey six months earlier, and duly appeared for trail at the Old Bailey before Mr. Justice Hilbery, who, after Nevin Craig had been found guilty, addressed him in a severe tone.

"Now I have heard your record," said the judge, "I am confirmed in the view that you are a very exceptionally determined man. You are not only cold-blooded, but from my observation of you I have not the least hesitation in saying I believe that you would shoot down, if you had the opportunity to do so, any police officer who was attempting to arrest you or, indeed, any lawful citizen who tired to prevent you from committing some felony which you had in mind."

The judge continued, "I think you would do it absolutely coldly, utterly regardless of the pain you might inflict. I am not at all sure that you ought not have had more than the other men concerned in that robbery, for this reason—I am sure you were the organizer, if not the leader. I have little doubt that it was you who held the gun and that these others were men of rougher material acting under your directions. You will go to prison for twelve years."

Nevin Scott Craig's mother left the Old Bailey sobbing, supported by her younger son, who had no tears but whose face was drawn with youthful bitterness and anger. He had lost his family hero. Moreover, he and other members of the Craig family did not believe that the elder son had been guilty of the crime for which he had been sent to prison.

Without the knowledge of his parents, Christopher Craig had forced his way into a house in South Croydon thirteen days before, accompanied by another youth. Both boys had revolvers supplied by Christopher Craig, and with them had threatened an elderly couple, from whom they had stolen about five pounds after knocking the woman down and threatening to tie up her husband. The episode had been an attempt to get back at a social system that had removed Nevin Craig from circulation, and of demonstrating to the younger brother that he was not the illiterate fool some of his schoolteachers considered him to be.

Two weeks later the exhilaration of that anti-social escapade had worn off. On October 31 Mr. Justice Hilbery sentenced the teenager's sibling hero to jail. The sixteen-year-old Christopher Craig was suddenly in isolation, and he felt vindictive against the police responsible for his brother's capture.

October 31 was a Friday. Within forty-eight hours of helping his tearful mother leave the Old Bailey, Christopher Craig had formulated a fresh means of taking revenge. He called at the home of an older youth whom he had known at school. The door was opened by the youth's mother, who did not approve of her son's association with the younger boy. She told Craig that her son was out. This wasn't true. He was watching television. Later, when he left the house in the company of two other callers, he saw Craig waiting for him.

"Hello, Derek," said the younger boy. "I've got something to say to you."

He did not know it, but when he heard those words spoken to him outside a newsagent's shop on a dark wet Sunday night Derek William Bentley, nineteen years old, was listening to the voice of doom. A few minutes later he caught a bus headed in the Croydon direction. Craig sat beside him and began to talk in a low voice very earnestly.

They left the bus at West Croydon station, crossed the main road, and started down a road skirting the shopping center and leading towards Waddon and Sutton. The nameplate on the wall they passed held the words "Tamworth Road". The time was about nine o'clock.

A quarter-of-an-hour later a woman who lived in Tamworth Road took her small daughter upstairs to put her to bed. As she reached up to draw the curtains she saw two figures across the road standing talking outside the premises of a firm called Barlow and Parker, wholesale confectioners. The woman at the window saw them turn their faces away from the lights of a passing bus, and when it had gone one of the loiterers became swiftly active. He sprang at the warehouse gate, hauled himself over, and dropped on the far side. The other was about to follow, but an approaching car caused him to turn away again and wait until it had passed. Then he followed his companion.

The woman ran to call her husband. When he heard what she

had seen he went out to phone the police, for there was no telephone in his home.

His phone call was switched through to Detective Frederick Fairfax, who was spending his Sunday evening in Croydon police station typing a report on a gas-meter theft. Fairfax left his typewriter, hurried into the station yard and collected another police officer named Harrison who was coming on duty. The pair climbed into a police van with some other officers and drove to Tamworth Road.

Meantime a radio call had alerted the driver of a patrol car cruising along London Road, down which Craig and Bentley had travelled by bus. Sidney Miles had put in twenty-two years as a constable in the Metropolitan Police and was looking forward to retirement on pension in a brief three years. That night as he drove Constable James McDonald, the radio operator of patrol car YZ, he was standing in for a colleague with whom he had swapped duty hours. As he drove to Tamworth Road the van from the station arrived outside the warehouse and Fairfax had a quick word with the woman who had watched the intruders scale the warehouse gate, then followed them and dropped into a narrow way that ran the length of the warehouse. Within a short time he was joined by McDonald. Fairfax had no flashlight, and the area behind the gate was dark. The detective decided to climb a drainpipe to reach a flat roof with several skylights. He reached it and caught a glimpse of two shadowy figures. He walked towards them calling, "I am a police officer."

"If you want us, come and get us," replied one, swearing.

Fairfax sprang forward and grabbed the taller, who was Bentley, and pushed him towards a stack that was the head of the warehouse elevator shaft. The detective later described what happened.

"As we got to the corner of the stack," he related, "Bentley broke away from me and as he did so he shouted, 'Let him have it, Chris.' There was a flash and a loud report, and I felt something strike my right shoulder which caused me to spin round and fall to the ground. As I was getting up I saw one person moving away from me to my left and one person moving to my right. I made a grab at the fellow on my right and found that I had again got hold of Bentley. I struck him with my fist and he fell to the ground. As he did so there was a second loud report and then I pulled Bentley up in front of me as a shield."

While this was taking place, McDonald had failed to climb up the stackpipe, being a more bulky man than Fairfax. But he heard the shots and the cry of "Let him have it, Chris." Harrison, the officer who had been coming on duty when Fairfax collected him, had made his way round the warehouse to Upper Drayton Place, where he climbed into the garden of a house in Tamworth Road. From there he climbed a part of the warehouse guttering until he could see that flat roof. He too heard Bentley call out, "Let him have it, Chris." Craig saw Harrison and fired two shots in his direction. Harrison moved back out of line of fire.

By this time armed police had arrived. They moved inside the warehouse and up a staircase that opened on to the flat roof. The first man out was Miles, the patrol car driver who had taken over another man's duty period. As he stepped forward on to the leads of the flat roof there was another shot. Miles went down as though poleaxed, shot through the head.

Harrison came after Miles, saw Craig with a pistol grasped in both hands. First the angry policeman threw his club, which Craig ducked, then a bottle of milk he had picked up, and followed that with a block of wood. Harrison said later that the figure with the gun fired at him before shouting, "I'm Craig. You've just given my brother twelve years. Come on, you coppers, I'm only sixteen."

Harrison remained there watching the angry youth, helpless while Craig held the gun. Fairfax took his prisoner down the staircase and returned to the roof with a revolver. He fired twice in the direction of Craig, who called to him, "You're going to make a shooting match of it, are you? Come on then, copper, let's have it out."

As he finished speaking he squeezed off another shot at the detective he had already wounded. Again he flaunted his contempt for the police.

"Come on, brave coppers, think of your wives!"

Fairfax moved closer and saw Craig take aim again. The detective heard the click of the hammer on an empty chamber.

There was a second and similar click, and Craig called, "See, it's empty."

Before Fairfax could close with him he darted to the edge of the roof. He leaped over, shouting, "Give my love to . . ." The rush of night air in his face as he fell made the last word indistinct, though it sounded like a girl's name, some of his hearers said later. Glass shattered as the empty gun hit a greenhouse and Craig's body smacked against the ground like a weighted sack. He muttered some swear words as a policeman landed on his back. But there was no further need for violence. Christoper Craig was through making his stand against the men he felt were responsible for his brother's imprisonment. He was taken to hospital, where it was found he had fractured his spine and his left forearm and also broken his breastbone in that wild leap from the roof.

While a surgeon worked on Craig's badly misused body, Bentley sat in Croydon police station making a statement, giving his version of the tragic episode. In that statement he said: "I knew we were going to break into the place. I did not know what we were going to get—just anything that was going. I did not have a gun and I did not know that Chris had one until he shot. I now know that the policeman in uniform that was shot is dead."

When, some time later, he was informed that he was to be charged with being concerned in the murder of Miles, Bentley looked shocked and said, "Chris shot him. I hadn't a gun. He was with me on the roof and shot him between the eyes."

It was a not quite coherent protest from a teenager who had suddenly awakened to the truth of what the night's events could mean to him personally.

In the Croydon hospital where he lay patched up and under sedation, Craig fought his way back to blurred consciousness and saw a policeman sitting beside his bed.

"Did I really kill a policeman?" he muttered, and then his train of thought switched, for he added, "I got the gun from a house in Purley. There are plenty more where that came from."

He was still challenging the law that had defeated his brother, even while under the effect of pain-killing drugs.

On the afternoon of Monday, November 3, he underwent an operation. As soon as he had recovered from the anaesthetic he was again voicing his hate.

"You coppers!" he gasped. "The other one's dead with a hole in his head. I'm all right. All you bastards should be dead."

On Thursday, November 6, he admitted the hatred he felt. He

watched a police officer write down his words as he forced them between his teeth: "If I hadn't cut a bit off the barrel of my gun I would probably have killed a lot more policemen. That night I was out to kill because I had so much hate inside me for what they did to my brother."

When Craig was taken by ambulance to be remanded by the local magistrate, he again saw tears in his mother's eyes. This time for him. It took a dozen policemen to keep back the hostile crowd when he was borne back to the ambulance. There were calls to kill the teenager who had thrown himself from a roof when blinded by rage and perhaps panic, or even a dawning sense of futility.

Whatever one's feelings about the savagery of Christopher Craig, or of the circumstances that conspired to make him into the youthful figure of violence that awed all Britain, there can be no doubt that he was utterly miserable within himself. His violence had solved nothing.

On the other hand, it had doomed the older youth whom he had taken along more or less for the ride and to provide company.

The trial of the teenagers for murder done on that warehouse roof in Croydon opened little more than a month later, on December 9, before Lord Goddard, who took his seat on the Bench precisely at half-past ten. Craig, parts of him in plaster, wore a new sports jacket and dark flannel trousers because his counsel had objected to his normal attire. It made him look too much like an American gangster. He shared the dock with Derek Bentley.

Both prisoners pleaded not guilty to the charge of murdering Sidney George Miles. Lord Goddard's glance swept towards them. He told Craig he could be seated. Bentley remained standing.

Christmas Humphreys opened for the Crown, and stated succinctly: "The case for the prosecution is this—that Craig deliberately and wilfully murdered that police constable and thereafter gloried in the murder; that Bentley incited Craig to begin the shooting and, although technically under arrest at the actual time of the killing of Miles, was party to that murder and equally responsible in law."

Thereafter there could be no mistaking the intentions of

counsel for the Crown. Age was not to influence the prosecution in placing legal guilt where it belonged. The dual defense of the prisoners in the dock was faced with a problem that was to prove insoluble except one way.

Craig, after his time in hospital, had recovered his thinly veiled animosity for the police. Fairfax, who had been promoted to sergeant since the shooting, was called to give his testimony as one of the foremost witnesses for the prosecution. When later Craig was accompanied down the steps of the dock to the cells below the court he told one of the guards he wished he had killed Fairfax as well.

At sixteen years of age he was not only incorrigible. He was a difficult youth to defend in his own interests. His counsel was adopting the line that, although he had fired the revolver on the fatal night, he had not deliberately aimed to kill or wound a policeman. He had been firing to hold them at bay.

Craig did little to help in his own defense.

He went into the witness-box and claimed he had told Bentley he had a gun and ammunition for it before he started shooting. He also denied that Bentley had told him not to use the gun. This was tearing apart Bentley's defense, which was that he had no knowledge of his companion being armed with a firearm until the shooting started.

There followed a good deal of legal sparring between counsel, in which the judge joined, as to how certain rulings in the past that seemed relevant to the present case should be viewed and interpreted. Some of this was undertaken with the jury absent so that they should not be unduly influenced by what they heard. But Craig's counsel won a partial victory in their absence by bringing Lord Goddard to agree that the alternative verdict of manslaughter should be left open to the jury.

When he addressed them the judge quickly impressed on the jury the need for approaching what he called "a very terrible case" in a calm frame of mind. He went through the evidence in a rather heavy manner, and closed his summation by declaring: "You owe a duty to the prisoners. You will remember and realize, I know, that you owe a duty to the community. If these young—but not so young that they are not responsible in law—men commit crimes of this sort, it is right, quite independently of any punishment, that they should be convicted."

After a pause he added, "Unless you find good ground for not convicting them it is your duty to do it, if you are satisfied with the evidence of the prosecution."

The jury wished to see Sergeant Fairfax's coat and waistcoat which had been ripped by the bullet that wounded his shoulder. Lord Goddard agreed that they should be accommodated, and the garments were produced and handed to the jury. At the same time they received a word of caution from the vigilant judge.

"You will remember, of course, gentlemen," he said, "you are not considering the wounding of Sergeant Fairfax. You are considering the death of Police Constable Miles."

The jury retired at a quarter past eleven in the morning. They returned to their places in the jury box by half-past twelve, in good time for lunch.

The foreman rose and told the court they found the prisoners guilty as charged. He added that the jury wished to add a recommendation to mercy in the case of Bentley.

The judge addressed the two teenagers in the dock. His first words were spoken to the older youth.

"Derek William Bentley," he said, "you are nineteen years of age. It is my duty to pass upon you the only sentence which the law can pass for the crime of wilful murder. The sentence of the court upon you is that you be taken from this place to a lawful prison, and thence to a place of execution, and there you suffer death by hanging, and that your body be buried within the precincts of the prison in which you shall have been last confined before your execution. And may the Lord have mercy on your soul."

He added to the attendant warders, "Take him down."

With Bentley gone, Craig stood alone in the dock to face the judge, who had removed from his wig the black square of silk called the black cap by ancient tradition.

His next words were spoken to the defiant Craig.

"Christopher Craig," he said, "you are under nineteen, but in my judgment and evidently in the judgment of the jury you are the more guilty of the two. Your heart was filled with hate, and you murdered a policeman without thought of his wife, his family, or himself, and never once have you expressed a word of sorrow for what you have done. I can only sentence you to be detained until Her Majesty's pleasure be known."

In effect, though Craig was receiving a sentence of life imprisonment, it might amount to about twenty-one years, if he were a good prisoner while serving the sentence and received time off for good behavior.

Lord Goddard added, "I shall tell the Secretary of State when forwarding the recommendation of the jury in Bentley's case that, in my opinion, you are one of the most dangerous young criminals who has ever stood in that dock."

The dock was the one in Number Two Court at the Old Bailey.

The judge concluded: "While the jury were out considering their verdict in this case, I had to deal with another case in which you were concerned with another boy whom you led into it, holding up an elderly couple at the point of revolvers and stealing from them—and it is quite obvious that the people in this country will not be safe if you are out of prison. I shall recommend the time which I suggest to the Secretary of State that you be kept in strict custody until the pleasure of Her Majesty be known."

Another glance at Craig's custodians, followed by a terse "Take him down," closed the notable dual murder trail in Court Number Two.

Craig's counsel did not advise his client to appeal against the verdict, but Bentley's did, and his appeal was heard in January of the following year.

The hub of the appeal, round which his case revolved, was that he had not called out, "Let him have it, Chris." But on the general showing of the evidence in the case, the appeal was turned down by the three judges hearing it. Not long afterwards the Home Secretary, Sir David Maxwell Fyfe, who had performed so ably for Britain at the Nuremberg trial, made a statement that, despite the Old Bailey jury's recommendation to mercy, he did not find sufficient reason to commute Bentley's sentence of death.

This refusal to act on the jury's recommendation evoked a public outcry on Bentley's behalf. There was an attempt to get a motion on the case heard in the House of Commons, for a number of Members were perturbed at the seeming disparity in the sentences due solely to age. Craig, who had fired the fatal shot, was not being hanged. Bentley, who some claimed was actually held under arrest at the time of the shooting, was to be hanged for a killing in which he had no physical part, despite that alleged encouraging cry to the youth with the murder weapon. The motion to hear the sentences debated was placed on the Order Paper, but removed on instructions from the Speaker, whereupon two MPs, Aneurin Bevan and Sir Lynn Ungoed-Thomas, the latter a former Solicitor-General, led a deputation to the Home Secretary. They endeavored to get him to change his mind. They did not succeed.

Derek Bentley was hanged at Wandsworth on January 28, 1953. Outside the prison gates a crowd of five hundred had collected to protest against the execution. After protesting they sang hymns. When at last a prison officer came out and pinned up a notice stating that the execution had taken place, the crowd dispersed.

But the case of the teenagers on a roof where a policeman was shot dead was not to be forgotten. It was vividly recalled at the time when the Royal Commission on Capital Punishment was taking evidence, and it may be that the case of the youth who was hanged for a shooting done by someone younger than himself carried considerable weight.

THE GREAT TRAIN ROBBERS

At the end of the first week of January 1970 television viewers in Britain were shown a piece of film of a man and two women on a bathing beach in Spain. The name of the man was Ronald Arthur Biggs. A few years before he had been a carpenter living in Alpine Road, Redhill. In 1970 the world was being combed for him, especially Australia, where he had arrived with his wife and family after a daring prison escape in England. On Thursday, April 16, 1964, he had stood with a number of other solemn-faced men in the spike-topped mahogany dock of the courtroom in Aylesbury and heard Mr. Justice Edmund Davies sentence him to thirty years' imprisonment after calling him a specious and facile liar who had that week perjured himself time and again.

He was the fourth of the ten prisoners in the dock at Aylesbury Assizes that day to be sentenced by the learned judge. Collectively they were known as the Great Train Robbers. They were the conspirators who had planned to rob a train of nearly two and a half million pounds in sterling, had brought off their daring *coup*, and somehow spirited away the proceeds of their intrepid robbery which had weighed one and three-quarter tons. Before that daring and successful robbery, all others faded in significance. The only difficulty for the robbers was how to remain at liberty once they had performed their holdup, which made the exploits of the notorious Jesse James, almost a century earlier, read like a game planned by a precocious child.

The holdup occurred at three o'clock in the morning of Thursday, August 8, 1963. The spot chosen was a lonely part of Buckinghamshire. The train held up and looted was the Royal Mail which had left platform eleven at Glasgow Central Station just before seven o'clock the previous summer evening. Following the early August bank holiday, the train was taking to London a special consignment of unwanted English banknotes, which had been brought across the Border into Scotland by English holiday tourists. The banknotes were acceptable as currency in Scotland, but were not used by the Scottish banks, which only paid out Scottish banknotes. For years past this habit of returning to England after the early August bank holiday the English banknotes that had found their way eventually into Scottish banks had been closely observed. Always the notes had been packaged and dispatched by the evening mail train to leave Glasgow on the Wednesday after the bank holiday Monday.

The habit was not generally known except to bankers and others concerned with clearing the English banknotes from cluttering up Scottish tills and safes. But it was a habit that had encouraged a group of plotters to devise a way of stopping the mail train and removing the bags containing the returned English banknotes, all used, with numbers that were unlisted.

When the currency bags were loaded on to the Glasgow-London train the value of the notes they contained amounted to more than two and a half million pounds sterling. The bags were consigned to the care of the travelling post office which accompanied the train.

Seventy Post Office sorters and their aides locked themselves in a dozen special coaches making up the train. One of the coaches was designated a high-value coach, which was customarily placed behind the first coach after the engine. Five Post Office workers were locked inside that coach. To keep them company they had a vast fortune in English banknotes secured in a hundred mailbags with distinctive markings.

On the way to London additional Post Office bags were to be taken aboard the train at Carlisle, Crewe, and Rugby. Indeed, that night so many mailbags were collected on the train that by the time it had cleared the Midlands some sixty or so bags were piled on the floor, impeding movements of the shirt-sleeved sorters. The Post Office coaches were fitted with self-locking devices for securing the doors that were considered burglarproof. For well over a century the money carried in the travelling post office had been collected and delivered at Euston Station, London, without hitch. Making that particular mail run had indeed become a habit, like any uninterrupted and well-regulated routine.

However, on that night, about thirty-nine miles northeast of its destination, the routine of more than a century was shattered. The point chosen for the holdup was a lonely section of the railway between Cheddington and Sears Crossing. An hour before the train was due to pass, a couple of Land Rovers and a large truck drove out of a farmyard sixteen miles away. The name of the farm was Leatherslade, and it was not only isolated but generally supposed to be deserted, two details that had influenced the leader of a gang of fifteen bandits who had planned the train robbery to choose it as a temporary headquarters.

The three vehicles carrying the armed robbers drove towards Bridego Bridge, near Cheddington, and turned off the road and parked. The fifteen men, each well primed and rehearsed in the part he had to play that night, walked away from their transport without using any giveaway flashlights. There was enough moonlight. Several made their way to where it had been decided the telephone lines would be severed, so that after the robbery there would be no easy means of communicating the news. One of the gang was a signals expert who had served time as a trainman. He walked nearly two-thirds of a mile along the line to the approach signal, which he disconnected. That done, he made his way to Sears Crossing, where he altered the signal circuits so that when a green light for "all clear" was supposed to be switched on, it showed a red light for "danger" instead.

All the fifteen members of the gang were dressed in used blue overalls of the kind worn by railway workers, and each had a signal flag for use in an emergency. When the train that was the target of so much conspiracy was heard approaching, it was travelling at close to eighty miles an hour. Well back from a suddenly glowing red-lit signal, fifteen pairs of ears strained and fifteen pairs of eyes scanned the distance up the line. Jack Mills of Crewe saw the red light and obediently braked, cutting the speed of his two thousand horsepower diesel. The Glasgow-London mail train, with wheels squealing, came to a gradual halt.

The driver turned to his fireman, David Whitby, also of Crewe but only half the driver's age, and told him to get down to the telephone box just up the line and phone through to the signal box to inquire how long the delay would be.

Whitby jumped from the train, ran to where Mills had said the line telephone would be, and put the instrument to his ear. It was dead. He looked at the wires and saw they had been cut.

He put down the useless phone, turned back to the train, and called to the driver, "Jack, the wires have been cut!"

It was as though those words were the cue awaited by the gang members concealed along the line. A man with a woollen helmet concealing his face suddenly jumped up beside Mills. In his right hand he swung a thick club wrapped in a cloth. Mills refused to be intimidated. He closed with the masked man threatening him with a club. A second man smashed a blow on his head from behind. As he went down to his knees both his attackers beat him over the head.

"Don't look up," one said threateningly, "or you'll get more."

The words came muffled through the mask over the speaker's face.

Whitby meanwhile had been pushed over a bank by a man in overalls who was carrying a signal flag. It was not until the man was close to him that the fireman realized the newcomer wore a balaclava helmet over his head. Whitby had no chance to save himself, for he was taken completely by surprise. As he landed at the bottom of the bank another masked phantom appeared with a raised blackjack in his fist.

"Shout and I'll kill you," he promised.

A bemused fireman was escorted back up the line to the stationary engine, where eight or nine masked gangsters stood over the prone driver, whose head was pouring blood over the floor of the cab. Both members of the driving crew were forced into a narrow passage behind the engine. This was the moment when the gang's train and signals expert was supposed to climb onto the engine and drive on. He came up and stared at the train's controls in consternation. They were completely new to him. He had never previously seen the controls of a 1B two thousand horsepower diesel.

The gang accordinly forced Mills under threats to drive the

train to Bridego Bridge, where he and his scared fireman were handcuffed together and forced to lie prone beside the tracks while an armed robber stood guard over them.

All this high drama had been accomplished without raising the suspicions of the Post Office workers in their coaches. They were well used to the trains on which they worked stopping and starting and shunting through the night-long journey of four hundred miles. It wasn't until a window of the high-value coach was beaten in, showering glass over the interior, that the men inside knew the train had been raided. Frank Dewhurst, the chief sorter, acted quickly and blocked the broken window with a couple of well-stuffed mailbags, at the same time calling to some of his men to lock the communicating door. There was no time. A man beat his way through with an axe. Other gangsters attacked Dewhurst from behind. In seconds, fifteen armed and determined raiders had overpowered the Post Office team and had them lying on the floor.

A gruff voice said, "You lot stay on the floor. We're leaving someone to make sure you don't move. God help you if you do."

Locks were smashed, wooden store cupboards smashed in, and the bags of money passed to others waiting to stack them in trucks parked under the bridge. Emptying the high-value coach of the bags of banknotes didn't take long, and then the men lying on the ground beside the track were forced up and into the coach where the five Post Office sorters were huddled. The seven men stared at one another. They were warned to stay there and do nothing for half an hour.

The gang members vanished. The men in the coach heard engines starting up and the sounds of vehicles pulling away. The chief sorter waited impatiently for about ten minutes, then left the coach. In amazement he saw that there was only the engine, the one coach behind it, and the high-value coach standing on the lines. The gang had uncoupled them before forcing Mills to drive to Bridego Bridge. Some miles away, in stationary coaches without an engine, Post Office sorters were still working at their piles of mail, getting it ready for delivery at Euston.

The raid had been, in its way, a fabulous success, brilliantly conceived and executed, almost like a military operation. Dewhurst came back and sent a couple of his men hurrying across the countryside to raise the alarm. They woke up a farmer who had no telephone but loaned one of the men his bicycle and sent him pedalling to Linslade.

However, the signalman at Cheddington, puzzled by the nonappearance of the expected mail train, had phoned Leighton Buzzard and been told the train had passed through that town half an hour earlier. He sent a parcels train to make a search down the line.

Within a few hours of Jack Mills having his head wounds dressed in the Royal Bucks Hospital in Aylesbury, the Postmaster-General, Reginald Bevins, was flying back from a holiday in Spain. He arrived in London to find that Scotland Yard was preparing to mount a mammoth manhunt for the audacious gangsters. The clue they hoped to discover was eventually provided by a herdsman who had worked only a mile from Leatherslade Farm. He had been suspicious of people he had seen calling at the supposedly deserted farm, which he had learned had been sold very recently. Four days after the robbery he walked over to Leatherslade and saw a truck with a tarpaulin over it. The farmhouse appeared deserted. Another truck stood in the yard. He left and phoned the police in Aylesbury. When they arrived at the farm they found not only the two trucks but a couple of Land Rovers. Blankets were draped over the farmhouse windows and beyond a row of runner beans was a pit. This hole was about five feet deep. Empty mailbags had been dumped in its clay. Similar bags were found inside the farmhouse and in a cellar was a heap of wrapping paper overprinted with "National Provincial Bank." The place was empty of furniture, but there were food stocks in the kitchen and the remains of a meal on the table. Cigarette-ends littered every room. To Leatherslade came Commander George Hatherill, head of the Yard's CID, with twenty picked detectives. They took the place apart, discovered overlooked fingerprints, loose floorboards where the gang's loot had been stored before they had decided to leave in a hurry, like men who had panicked, and carefully collected the scattered pieces of a game of Monopoly.

The detectives were surprised. After all the care that had gone to planning and to putting into operation the actual robbery, the men who had lifted two and a half million pounds had suddenly behaved like scared sneak thieves.

The experienced detectives took hope from this sign of panic.

Panicky men lacked caution, and lack of caution pointed to men who might behave like amateurs. This proved right thinking, for the first success in rounding up the gang came about when a policeman's widow in Bournemouth became suspicious because two men who wished to rent a garage from her insisted on paying three months' rent in advance—and in used notes.

She phoned the police and within a short time Roger John Cordrey and William Gerald Boal were in custody after putting up a fight. In the van they had brought to the garage was found a pile of paper money amounting to £141,017. When Boal's wife was visited by police she showed them where she had put £330 given to her by her husband. Checking on Cordrey sent detectives to East Molesey, where a husband and wife named Pilgrim, the owners of a florist shop, were talked into delivering up £860 in five-pound notes.

The tide was turning.

The five arrested persons were taken to Linslade the next day to appear before a Buckingham magistrate. They were in court when a young couple roaming through Redland Wood, at Box Hill in Surrey, found a briefcase and two suitcases lying near the path. When they opened the bags they stared at £101,000 in banknotes, some of the proceeds of the mail train robbery.

Obviously the gang's panic was increasing. The next weekend wooded areas around London were invaded by hundreds of hopeful explorers looking for more of the train loot. The next development was the identifying of a man and woman who had abandoned a car at Hayes, Essex, as an antique dealer named Bruce Richard Reynolds and Mrs. Mary Kazih Manson. The woman was found, but she could not tell the police where Reynolds had vanished. By this time the police were also looking for a James White whom they believed had hurriedly left a trailer on a site only a few miles from where the money was found on Box Hill. Secreted in the walls were £30,000 in banknotes.

It was the arrest of a bookmaker named Charles Frederick Wilson that gave the manhunt a touch of color. When questioned by Superintendent Butler he admitted having made a "ricket," underworld slang for a bad error. Then he told the superintendent with an air of confidence, "I don't see how you can make it stick without the poppy—and you won't find that."

"Poppy" was underworld slang for cash. Wilson, however,

was both right and wrong. The greater amount of the stolen money has not been found. But the case against him was made to "stick" when the bookmaker from Clapham eventually found himself in court.

Other detectives arrested Brian Arthur Field, a clerk employed by the lawyers who arranged the sale of Leatherslade Farm to a nominee of the gang. A seaman named Field, who was no relation to the clerk, was arrested on the same day. After the trial they each received a sentence of twenty-five years.

Perhaps the most spectacular character questioned closely by the police was Douglas Gordon Goody, who owned a women's hairdressing salon in Putney. Two years before he had been arrested for taking part in a wages robbery at London Airport, but had been acquitted during the trial after he had established an alibi. In connection with the train robbery he made several trips to Aylesbury to talk to the police.

After one of the trips in his white sports car he told waiting reporters, "I have nothing to do with it at all. I don't mind it so much for myself, but there's my mother to think of. When she looks out of the window, the chances are there's a detective outside. When I go out, it's a certainty one is following me. Anyone would think I was one of the train robbers."

Not long afterwards he was arrested and charged and eventually took his place with the others during the trial that lasted for a quarter of a year. When Mr. Justice Davies addressed him before sentencing him he told Goody: "In some respects you present this court with one of the saddest problems by which it is confronted in this trial. You have manifest gifts of personality and intelligence which could have carried you far had they been directed honestly. I have not seen you in court for three months without noticing that you are a man capable of inspiring the admiration of your fellow accused."

He was sentenced to thirty years.

Brian Field's employer was arrested and charged with harboring one of the suspected robbers, but in his case he was allowed bail in the sum of £15,000. He was the last of the associated gang to be found guilty and sentenced. He went to prison for three years.

After his arrest the police unmasked the missing Bruce Reynolds's brother-in-law, John Thomas Daly, who had grown a beard and adopted the name of Grant. The police claimed he had been traced through fingerprints left at Leatherslade, though he denied, when captured, that he had ever been to the farm. A week after he had been taken into custody another suspect was arrested in St. John's Wood after a rooftop chase. This prisoner was Roy John James, nicknamed the Weasel. He was a racing driver whose Brabham Ford was familiar on some tracks. It was after his capture that Scotland Yard received a phone call by someone who refused to be identified. A telephone booth was visited and inside were found two sacks. They contained £50,000 of the missing money. Up to that time about £300,000 had been recovered. Well over two millions still remained to be accounted for, and the most wanted suspect was Bruce Reynolds, who was reported to have reached the continent and employed the services of a plastic surgeon.

Meanwhile in Buckinghamshire, where the arrested suspects had to be taken to be formally charged, the owner of Leatherslade Farm had had returned to him the property he had sold for £5,500. He invited the interested general public to look over the one-time hideout of the now notorious gang at half-a-crown a head.

The trial of those arrested opened on January 20, 1964, in a court that had been provided by Aylesbury's adapted Rural District Council offices. The twenty prisoners comprised seventeen men and three women. Double that number of counsel were present, including a dozen Queen's Counsels. For convenience, eight of the prisoners were removed from the overcrowded dock. They were to be tried later. The twelve who remained all pleaded not guilty.

There was an early sensation when one counsel rose and suggested he had reason to believe the jury might have been tampered with. It was Superintendent Butler and the judge himself who allayed the court's fears about intimidation. Once the trial had passed through the somewhat formal opening stages there was excitement created by the evidence of the Yard's fingerprint expert, Superintendent Maurice Ray. One prisoner named Hussey had left a palm-print on the tailboard of a truck at Leatherslade; another Thomas Wisbey, had left his fingerprints on a rail in the bathroom; while Daly's prints were on pieces from a game of Monopoly used to while away the long hours of waiting. Another prisoner named Welch had left a palm-print on a beer can. Wilson had been even more careless, for he had left a thumb-print on a salt container, a similar print on some wrapping, and palm-prints on a windowsill. The Weasel's "dabs" were on a dish in which a cat had been given its food, while the prisoner Brian Field was amazed to hear that he had left his fingers' secret signature on the suitcases found at Box Hill.

By that time Ronald Biggs had been removed from the dock to be tried later. Even more startling was the later discharge of John Thomas Daly after the jury had been dismissed for two days. His counsel had submitted that he had no case to answer. Mr. Justice Davies, after due consideration, agreed; and when the jury returned he told the court, "It would not be right for the case against Daly to proceed any further. Suspicion alone is quite insufficient." So the missing Bruce Reynolds's brother-in-law was duly discharged. His clothes fitted him badly, for he had lost about 28 pounds during the past months.

The trial continued with ten men in the dock. Their array of counsel did their best in circumstances offering little scope, and it came time for the judge to sum up. His Welsh lilt continued with persuasive calm for more than thirty hours, at the end of which time he told the jury they were virtually prisoners until they had reached a verdict.

The jury retired on Monday, March 23, were three days deliberating, and returned to court in the morning of Thursday, March 26. They had been prisoners of the court for nearly sixty-six and a half hours, and their retirement created a record, for it was the longest undertaken by any British jury.

The prisoners in the dock were called individually to face the jury. The first was William Boal.

"Do you find him guilty of being a robber or receiver?" said the clerk of the court. "Just answer yes or no."

"Yes," said the foreman.

The other convicted train robbers were Wilson, Wisbey, Welch, Hussey, James, and Goody. Brian Field was found guilty of being a conspirator to rob and guilty of conspiring with his name-sake and his employer to conceal the identity of the purchaser of Leatherslade Farm and to obstructing the course of justice. He was found not guilty of being a train robber and receiving £100,900.

On April 8, the remaining prisoners were tried. That was after the first trial had lasted through fifty-one working days and the evidence of two hundred and sixty-four witnesses had been heard. It was assessed that two and a half million words had been spoken in court, one for each pound of the money stolen that memorable August night in the previous year.

The first was Biggs. On the 9th his trial was transferred to the regular assize-court building. He was another whose fingerprints had been found at the farm, but he claimed he had gone there with a friend to enquire about what he called "a big enterprise." When he and his friend discovered what was being planned, they left. The friend who could have provided him with his alibi did not turn up in court. The jury found Biggs, in the foreman's words, "Guilty on both charges."

On April 16, Mr. Justice Davies delivered his sentences on the convicted robbers. He told Cordrey, the first to be called: "You are the first to be sentenced out of eleven greedy men whom hope of gain allured. You and your co-conspirators have been convicted of complicity in one way or another, of a crime which in its impudence and enormity is the first of its kind in this country. I propose to do all in my power to ensure it will also be the last of its kind."

The court was very still after these words.

The learned judge continued his survey of the crime and the criminals until he said, "After mature deliberation, I propose to treat you all in the same manner, with two exceptions."

Cordrey was informed he was the first of the exceptions. Because he had admitted his guilt and had helped the police to recover nearly £80,000, he was going to prison for twenty years.

That brought gasps from those listening. If that was leniency, what kind of sentences had Judge Davies in mind for the others?

The second exception was William Boal, aged fifty and the oldest man in the dock. The judge recalled that he had begged for mercy. He was accorded it in the sentence of twenty-four years in jail.

Again the court gasped.

But after Charles Wilson was sentenced to thirty years there was only silence in the court. It was the silence of profound shock. Biggs and the others who followed took their thirty-year sentences like men in a daze. But not Hussey, known as Big Jim. His natural resilience of temperament allowed him to get in the last word when, after being sentenced, he said mockingly, "Thank you, my lord."

With the sentencing of the robbers over, time still had to be found for trying those charged with receiving. This took an additional couple of days. The Pilgrims, husband and wife, and Mrs. Boal had pleaded not guilty to receiving £860 and £330. They were acquitted, while a mechanic who had pleaded guilty to receiving £545 was accorded a conditional discharge. A man who had admitted receiving £2,000 was sentenced to three years, but his wife who had denied receiving £450 was acquitted. A driver who admitted receiving £518 was sent to jail for twelve months.

The historically heavy sentences created much comment and even criticism, for they marked a fresh landmark in penal punishment for the criminal in the modern age. However, it took more than four years for the missing Bruce Reynolds to be brought to justice for his part in the Great Train Robbery. He was captured in Torquay. When he was tried at Buckinghamshire Assizes in January 1969 before Mr. Justice Thompson, he too learned that his fingerprints left at Leatherslade had betrayed him to the police. He had been another who had sat down to while away the time with a game of Monopoly. His trial was in effect a formality, for he had pleaded guilty after being captured and had made restitution of a sum amounting to about £6,500. He had also expressed his regret for the violence that had occurred during the hold-up.

When Mr. Justice Thompson sentenced the prisoner he said: "It would be wrong for me to give any encouragement to the idea that successful avoidance of arrest for a period entitles a criminal to a reduction in sentence." He then recalled Reynolds's repayment of the money, his expression of contrition for the suffering caused, and the fact that he had pleaded guilty, and recalled what Mr. Justice Davies's comments had been at the time of the main trial. He added: "I shall make the same kind of reduction in sentence as I believe would, in like circumstances, have been made by the judge at the main trial. I sentence you to twenty-five years' imprisonment."

Superintendent Butler, the detective who had made it his career to nab the train robbers was asked by reporters when he left the court that January day if he now considered the case closed.

He gave a quick shake of his head and said, "Got to find Biggs first," and turned away, a man who considered he still had a job to complete since Biggs had daringly escaped from the British prison where he had been confined. Charles Wilson, another who had made a successful prison break, had been captured in Canada.

Nine months later, in mid-October 1969, the last known train robber to be enjoying his freedom made the headlines again. He had been narrowly missed by Melbourne police who had uncovered his hideout in Hibiscus Street, where he had been living a new life with his family under an assumed name.

With Biggs again on the run what was described as the biggest manhunt in Australia's history got under way. The fugitive's resources were slender. Whatever had happened to the missing bulk of the stolen proceeds of the Great Train Robbery, Ronald Biggs had little enough, according to his wife, when he took a hurriedly filled suitcase and vanished before the police arrived in Hibiscus Street.

"He had forty dollars in his pocket," she told the Australian detectives who questioned her.

Forty Australian dollars are about eighteen pounds sterling.

Apparently the panic that overcame the gang in Leatherslade Farm had not been stilled after more than five years and more than twelve thousand miles distant. Like the fear of eventual arrest, it was always waiting to keep company with a lonely man on the run, even after April 1970 when Tommy Butler, the "Gray Fox" of the Flying Squad, died in a London hospital, his task of finding and recapturing Ronald Biggs uncompleted.